"Every woman who is struggling to understand the mistreatment she is experiencing in her relationship should begin by reading the wonderful book *When Love Hurts*. In these pages she will find the strength, validation, and insight she needs to reclaim her life and return it to its rightful owner—her."　　—Lundy Bancroft, author of *Why Does He Do That?*

"This is an excellent resource, not only for women to use on their own, but also for counselors and advocates."
—Dr. Mary Russell, Professor of Social Work,
University of British Columbia

"I give a copy of *When Love Hurts* to every one of my clients. They all find it profoundly helpful. The book rings true. The authors show a deep and comprehensive understanding of what it is to live with abuse. Women say to me, 'This is my story! Only the names are different. How did they know?!'"
—Daphne Wilson, Woman Abuse Support Worker,
Powell River, British Columbia

"*When Love Hurts* is a great resource for any woman who is tired of taking the blame for a painful relationship. If you wonder why the man you love is hurting you—and what you can do about it—this book will give you all kinds of useful information and strategies for changing your life. Just as importantly, it makes it clear that you are not responsible for his abusive behavior."
—Jackson Katz, author of *The Macho Paradox:*
Why Some Men Hurt Women and How All Men Can Help

WHEN
LOVE
HURTS

A WOMAN'S GUIDE TO
UNDERSTANDING ABUSE IN RELATIONSHIPS

Jill Cory
AND
Karen McAndless-Davis

NEW AMERICAN LIBRARY
New York

NEW AMERICAN LIBRARY
Published by Berkley
An imprint of Penguin Random House LLC
375 Hudson Street, New York, New York 10014

Library of Congress Cataloging-in-Publication Data

Names: Cory, Jill, author. / McAndless-Davis, Karen, author.
Title: When love hurts : a woman's guide to understanding abuse in relationships / Jill Cory and Karen McAndless-Davis ; foreword by Lundy Bancroft.
Description: New York : NAL, 2016.
Identifiers: LCCN 2016014526 (print) | LCCN 2016017565 (ebook) | ISBN 9780425274286 (paperback) | ISBN 9780698155305 (ebook)
Subjects: LCSH: Love. | Interpersonal relations. | Spousal abuse. | BISAC: FAMILY & RELATIONSHIPS / Abuse / General. | FAMILY & RELATIONSHIPS / Abuse / Domestic Partner Abuse. | FAMILY & RELATIONSHIPS / Love & Romance.
Classification: LCC BF575.L8 C667 2016 (print) | LCC BF575.L8 (ebook) | DDC 362.82/92019—dc23
LC record available at https://lccn.loc.gov/2016014526

WomanKind Press edition / September 2000
WomanKind Press revised edition / February 2008
New American Library trade paperback edition / October 2016

Printed in the United States of America
1   3   5   7   9   10   8   6   4   2

Cover art by Shutterstock
Cover design by Rita Frangie
Book design by Kristin del Rosario

CONTENTS

Contents

- Why Does the End of a "Bad" Relationship
  Still Hurt So Much?
- Is It Always Going to Be This Painful?
- Can I Look Forward with Hope?

ABOUT THE AUTHORS

Jill Cory and Karen McAndless-Davis are friends and colleagues who share a deep compassion and respect for women who have experienced abuse. Together, they bring over four decades of experience to their work.

While Jill was in graduate school at the University of Calgary, she began working at a women's shelter. She was so moved by the strength of the women as they struggled to make sense of their partners' abusive behavior that she dedicated her career to supporting women with experiences of abuse. She moved to Vancouver in 1987 to pursue research at the University of British Columbia, exploring the barriers and challenges that women face when leaving abusive relationships. For the next seven years she developed and facilitated group counseling programs for women, and was part of a team that provided groups for abusive men. Jill has worked at BC Women's Hospital & Health Centre for eighteen years, traveling extensively to deliver violence-informed, women-centered workshops and seminars to improve health care and community services for women experiencing abuse. Jill lives with David, her partner of thirty-one years, and they have two adult children, Becky and Ben.

Karen's passion for this issue comes from personal experience. Her partner, Bruce, was abusive at the beginning of their marriage. After several years of hard work, Bruce changed his abusive behavior and the beliefs underlying his actions. Karen and Bruce have now been happily married in a relationship of trust and respect for over twenty-five years. Karen found being in a support group for women who have experienced abuse life changing. As things improved in her own life, she felt compelled to find ways to share what she learned with other women. For more than eighteen years now, she has provided individual and group counseling to women in various communities and has consulted with many communities to establish support groups for women. She also travels widely to provide training on the women-centered approach presented in *When Love Hurts*. Karen and Bruce have two children, Luke and Isaac.

ACKNOWLEDGMENTS

We thank all the women whom we have been privileged to know, support, and learn from. Your desire for a safer future has taught us about the strength of the human spirit and our infinite capacity to care for each other. We would like to express our deep gratitude to you. Your wisdom and courage have inspired us to tell your stories.

We also want to thank the women who contributed to this book by giving us their invaluable insights and suggestions. Your comments and encouragement motivated and guided us.

Since the conception of this book, Bruce McAndless-Davis has been an amazing supporter. The first edition of this book would not have become a reality without his constant encouragement and hundreds of hours of work. He has worn many hats through our adventures in self-publishing, including publishing manager, bookkeeper, and "tech guy." His dedication and support have been invaluable to us.

Special thanks to Sherwin Arnott at Pink Sheep Media for bringing his creativity, intelligence, and ethics to the design of the second edition of the book. Sherwin patiently and persistently led (dragged!) us into the world of social media, and we are glad for the connections to women that this has created.

Jill's acknowledgments: Karen, your wisdom and unwavering commitment to women's safety is a constant source of inspiration for me. What good fortune it has been for me to work and learn with you.

David, you have been my source of knowledge about respectful relationships between women and men. For that, I thank you deeply.

Karen's acknowledgments: Jill, your unfailing conviction that men and women can live in mutual, loving, and respectful relationships inspired Bruce and me to live and love in a way that is truly a gift. Your belief that I had something to offer other women was the inspiration I needed to get started in this work. The deep respect and compassion with which you approach every woman is an attitude I feel grateful to have made my own.

Bruce, there have been many times in my work that have felt impossible. You have been a constant voice to say, "Yes, you can!" Thank you.

FOREWORD

BY LUNDY BANCROFT

Hurt feelings. Rejection. Humiliation. Intimidation. Feeling stupid. Feeling violated. Confusion. Confusion. Confusion. These are the feelings that an abusive or controlling man causes in his partner over and over again during their relationship.

But only some of the time. Other days he makes her feel loved. And sexy. And special. And cared for. Her emotions get tossed all over the place on what feels like a stormy sea.

During certain periods, it seems like he's finally done with all the criticism and coldness. Your hopes can rise during these times, when it seems like all of his unkindness is gone for good. But then, bafflingly, it all suddenly swirls downward again. That razor-sharp look comes back into his eyes, and once again all he sees is a collection of things he claims are wrong with you. The ups and downs are exhausting, and they take their toll.

More than a decade has passed now since I wrote *Why Does He Do That?*, a book that set out to explain what goes on inside the minds of men who control and tear down their partners in these ways. During those years, I have been concerned that my book both said too much and didn't say enough. I tried as well as I could to answer the key questions that go through women's minds about their destructive partners: "Why is he so different from how he was early in our relationship?

Why does he seem to love me some days and other days he acts disgusted by me? What does he really want? Will he ever change?"

With a focus on abusive men's behavior, I ended up feeling unsure that I had spent enough time on a crucial question, the last and hardest one of all for a woman who is experiencing abuse: "What should I *do*, now that I understand what's wrong?"

Recently I discovered Jill Cory and Karen McAndless-Davis's amazing book, *When Love Hurts*, which you now hold in your hands. I don't have to feel bad anymore about the points that I couldn't devote enough attention to in my book; the wisdom here flies forward from the authors, who share the experiences of many hundreds of women. *When Love Hurts* is, simply, the best book I've ever read for women who are being chronically emotionally wounded in their relationships.

In these pages, you will find concrete, practical solutions to these challenges:

How do I make sense out of all the twists and turns in my partner's behavior?

How do I stop blaming myself for how he treats me?

How can I tell if he's going to change?

How can I keep myself safe?

How do I get control of my life back?

It's true that there is one question that the authors of *When Love Hurts* can't answer for you, which is whether you should leave your partner or not. But they offer tremendous help with making that decision *for yourself*, walking you step-by-step through the factors that you need to consider as you plan out the road ahead.

If I had to choose one negative effect that abusive men cause above all others, my answer would be "confusion." In fact, one of the warning signs that you're involved with an abusive partner is if you spend a lot of your time feeling baffled by what is going on and stressed about what will come next. Over time, confusion leads to paralysis; when you can't make sense of what is happening, you naturally tend to freeze up. It can become anxiety-producing to move in any direction, because you feel as though any way you go could be the wrong way. Women who have experienced abuse often feel that control over their own lives is slipping through their fingers.

When Love Hurts replaces confusion with clarity and paralysis with insight and an awareness of options. This is not a book that devotes huge space to analyzing what has gone wrong; it gives you just enough insight to make it possible for you to clear your mind. Then it moves on quickly to take on what matters most: the path you can take to get back to being in control of your own life. You will learn here how to break out of isolation; how to keep from getting drawn in each time your partner is having one of his good periods; how to rebuild your self-esteem; and how to heal from the harm he has done to your spirit.

Through this process it's possible that you will come to a place where you decide it's time to end your relationship. But you won't necessarily. What matters most is that you come out making your own choices, rather than feeling that they are being controlled by your partner or by fate. Your life should, and can, belong to you. And you will find a way to take it back.

I am wishing you all the best during this next phase in your life. The future is brightening just from the fact that you are holding *When Love Hurts* in your hands.

—Lundy Bancroft

WHY WE WROTE THIS BOOK

Prior to writing this book, we had both been leading support groups for women experiencing abuse from their partners. We saw how women's lives transformed when they had access to support and accurate information about abuse, and we were saddened to realize that this empowering material was not otherwise available to women. We knew that having the right information could make all the difference. In response, we wrote this book to help women answer the multitude of questions that come with living with an abusive partner. We took the material from our support groups and laid it out in a book, interspersing it with women's stories. Since we self-published our first edition in 2000, what we've heard most often from women is that this book has been lifesaving. We understand this sentiment on two levels: Having insight into abuse can literally save women's lives; and equally important, women tell us the book has "saved their sanity." Abuse can be so confusing, overwhelming, and isolating. Women often tell us that they feel like they are going crazy and the book helps them to see that they are not alone, not to blame, and not crazy.

I received this book when I was in a women's shelter. This book helped me understand what happened to me and why. It helped me realize I am not alone, and all my reactions—confusion, fear, anger, and sadness—are normal responses to being abused. This book should be given to every woman in the world who is experiencing abuse. I believe it is essential and makes the transition to recovery and freedom less scary. What I would say to other women is that I know how much it hurts, I know how scary it is, and that others on the outside do not always understand. This book gives you all the answers for yourself, and for your friends and family to help you through this. Be strong, you do deserve better and you are worth it.

—**TAMMY**

With encouragement and feedback from women, we published a second edition in 2008, adding new material. It has been so gratifying to see how many women have used our book to change their lives. From a modest beginning of self-publishing, we are now delighted that our book is being published by a major publishing house so that it can reach even more readers.

Since this book was first published, we have discovered it also has a wider audience. Professionals supporting women who have experienced abuse will find this book helpful. Reading this book will assist you to better understand the complex situation women find themselves in. Many counselors, advocates, and shelter workers find this book a great guide for both individual and group counseling. We also encourage doctors, lawyers, religious leaders, and others to keep a copy of this book available for their own reference and to loan to those seeking advice or direction.

Similarly, friends and family will find this a helpful book. When someone we love is being hurt in a relationship, there is a natural impulse to stop the hurt as quickly as possible. Friends and family may make the mistake of oversimplifying the situation and pushing the woman either to leave the relationship or to "fix" it. Unfortunately, there is nothing simple about all the conflicting emotions, potential risks, and practical challenges of living with an abusive man. What women need most are support people who appreciate how difficult their situation is and can hang in with them during the long run. This book can help you to be that kind of person.

All the stories in this book are true. Some of the stories are told of women; some of them are told by the women themselves. The names and identifying characteristics of all women have been changed to protect their privacy.

INTRODUCTION

Love is meant to be supportive. We expect our partners to provide strength and comfort to us. But what happens when love hurts? What if your partner betrays your love by hurting you through his words or actions? You may feel confused, angry, sad, or even depressed. It can be hard to know what to do or who to talk to. Perhaps you've told yourself, "My situation is not that bad," or "I'm exaggerating the problem." Maybe others have told you that your experiences are part of the normal ups and downs of a relationship. Maybe you think that the problem lies with you and you're the one who needs to change. You may have tried many times to make changes within your relationship, but you continue to be hurt.

We wrote this book for women who have experienced abuse from their current or past male partner.[1] If your partner has not physically hurt you, you may wonder if you have really been abused. Maybe others have suggested to you that if you haven't been hit, it's not really abuse. We do not think this is true. Women have taught us that all forms of abuse are devastating and so this book recognizes that there are many types of abuse, including verbal, emotional, financial, sexual, psychological, spiritual, and physical.

You've probably been feeling alone and overwhelmed, and we

---

1 While the main audience for this book is women with male partners, if you are in a same-sex relationship and are experiencing abuse, this material will also be helpful for you.

hope this book can be a companion on your journey. Women are used to being told by professionals, family, or friends what they "should" do. Women are advised to leave the relationship, change themselves, fix the relationship, or simply accept their partner's behavior. We believe you are the expert on your lives; only you know what is best and safest for you. Women have told us that this book provided them with a new way of understanding their situation. We are not suggesting you stay in your relationship, and we are not suggesting you leave. Our goal is to give you support and information so you can make sense of your experience and feel like you have some options.

In this book, you will meet other women who have been betrayed and hurt by their partners. You will hear these women describe the pain and confusion of their relationships and their journeys to find answers. We have included women's stories for two reasons. First, we want to help you, the reader, feel less alone. Many of the stories in this book will ring true for you. Up until now, you may have felt completely isolated in your situation. You are not. Second, we know that women learn from other women's experiences—drawing strength and insight from each other. We hope that, in hearing other women's stories, you will begin to hear your own story more clearly.

The exercises from our counseling program are also laid out in this book, and it is designed for you to write in. Recording your experiences can help you to clarify your thoughts. However, if you are still living with your partner, you may be concerned that he will find this book and use it against you. If this is a concern, you may decide not to include your personal thoughts. You may even want to hide the book entirely from your partner.

We encourage you to read this book at your own pace. Some women read this book quickly, feeling relieved to have finally found something that gives words to their experience. Other women read it slowly, wanting to absorb it bit by bit. Do what is right for you. If you start feeling overwhelmed or find the material difficult to read, it's okay to give yourself a break. If you have a trusted friend or professional, you might want to talk with them about what you are experiencing.

We want to say a word about safety. You might think of your safety as only physical safety. We always include both emotional and physical safety because they are equally important. Women have taught us that emotional abuse can also be very damaging and sometimes lead to unsafe and life-threatening situations. If you feel that you or your children are in danger, safety concerns need to come first. This might mean leaving the relationship, even if only for a while. Find a safe place, such as a women's shelter, where you can assess your safety and explore your options.

If you are being hurt by the person you love, the fact that you love him may no longer be enough. It takes tremendous courage to begin to ask deeper questions. We trust that this book will help you find answers as you search for a brighter and safer future.

—JILL CORY AND KAREN MCANDLESS-DAVIS

ALLISON'S STORY

We begin our book with one woman's story. "Allison" is not this woman's real name, but her experiences are real. You may see aspects of your own life reflected in hers. At the same time, we know that every woman is unique, and parts of Allison's story will not be familiar to you. We also know that the choices Allison made may not be your choices. Every woman finds her own solutions; these are Allison's solutions, and this is her story. You will do what is right for you, even if you don't know exactly what that is yet.

I met Paul on an airplane flight. We struck up a conversation, and he said, "Why don't we get together for dinner and a movie?" meaning that we should move to the center of the plane for the meal and film. I found this all very flattering. I thought to myself, "Here's this handsome, charming man talking to me. This is quite wonderful."

We talked for a long time on the plane, and I really enjoyed myself, but I also thought that after the flight we'd just go our separate ways as we lived in different cities. To my surprise, as the plane landed, he said he would be staying in town and asked if we could get together the following evening. We went out for dinner and a play. That night I stayed over at his hotel, which was very romantic. It all seemed so exciting. Looking back, though, I realize that it happened too quickly.

We started dating. He called me all the time and gave me small gifts and cards. No other man had ever treated me so nicely, and I felt swept off my feet. However, after a few months, I got a strange call from him in the middle of the night. He was drunk and started grilling me about why I hadn't answered his phone call earlier that day. This was my first indication that there was a problem. Still, it seemed to be an isolated event; I didn't want to make a big deal out of it.

We did lots of fun things together, but I always had an anxious feeling in the pit of my stomach. His interest in me was too intense and I had doubts about the relationship. When I expressed these concerns, Paul reassured me by saying, "Don't worry, my job is to win you over."

Paul put a lot of pressure on me to live with him, and he also asked me to marry him early on. It was very confusing—he seemed so committed, but at the same time I didn't like feeling pressured to move things along so quickly. He said he wanted to have children with me. This appealed to me as I was twenty-nine, I really wanted kids, and it seemed to be the right time in my life for a family.

While we were dating, I often felt frustrated. Paul never quite understood me; even when I explained things very carefully, he would misinterpret me. He would get angry and twist my words around. I remember once when I told him I wanted to slow the relationship down and he accused me of wanting to see other men. Looking back, this was a red flag, but I didn't see it at the time.

Conversations with him would leave me questioning my competence, my sanity. I felt like I put so much thought and effort into communicating, and he was always attacking me with his words. It was exhausting.

One night while I was driving us to a friend's party, we began arguing about what I was wearing, and all of a sudden he punched me on the leg. I stopped the car, and he started screaming. I was really frightened. He later apologized and said that he was just worried that other men would find me attractive. He promised it would never happen again. But it wasn't the last time. At other times during our relationship he would slap or punch me, and sometimes I would hit back. No one had ever hit me before, and I had certainly never hit anyone either. Now I see I was trying to defend myself, but at the time I felt like I was as bad as him.

We had been together for about ten months when I came down with what I thought was the flu. My body ached and I was exhausted all the time. I would drag myself to work but I don't know how I got anything done. And the slightest thing would make me cry. I remember one day my boss asked me to correct a mistake in a report I put together and I went back to my office and just fell apart. I finally went to the doctor and was diagnosed as being clinically depressed. She said that could be the cause of my recent weight gain—something Paul had begun criticizing me about. My doctor wrote a prescription for antidepressants and asked about what was going on in my life—with work and my relationship. I told her everything was fine. And I really knew it wasn't. Looking back now, I see that a lot of my depression was related to Paul.

Around this time, Paul and I also started to see a counselor. I thought we had a communication problem and that a counselor could help us. When I revealed that Paul had hit me, the counselor said he wouldn't work with couples if there was any violence. He told me that I had to stop pushing Paul's buttons and that Paul had to stop hitting me. Because the counselor was a professional, I wanted to take his advice. I tried to be more accommodating with Paul, but it never made any difference. (Even after we separated, Paul would use the counselor's words to blame me for "pushing his buttons" and causing the problems in our relationship.)

We just sort of ended up looking for a place to buy together. I had doubts about buying a home with Paul, but he was very persuasive. The day the deal went through, I found out I was pregnant. Getting pregnant was unexpected, but we were both pleased. It became very hard to say no to all of this—a new home, a baby, a partner. I knew I wanted these things in my life so I just tried to put my doubts aside. I thought, "These are my insecurities, and I just need to work through this."

Once we got into our own place, the fights escalated. One night during a disagreement, Paul started smashing a crystal tumbler against my head repeatedly. It was the first time he'd really hurt me. I probably needed stitches, but I didn't go to the hospital. I was fifteen weeks pregnant and felt emotionally and physically vulnerable. Going to the hospital would have just made things worse with Paul. I didn't tell anyone because I knew others would want me to leave, and I knew I wasn't going to. Now that I was pregnant, I thought, "I need to make this work."

When Alex was born, Paul was more supportive during labor than I'd ever hoped, staying with me during the entire labor, trying to make me comfortable and reassuring me when I was scared. But the next night he called me at the hospital very late. He screamed at me for talking so much to the midwife during the delivery and "flirting" with the doctor. His ranting was awful, but at the same time he did some very nice things like bring me flowers and my favorite chocolates. I was very confused.

Once we got home with the baby, it was all up to me. Paul never dressed, bathed, fed, or changed Alex. I had just assumed that Paul and I were in this together and was disappointed at his self-centeredness.

Even at this point, we still had lots of fun together but it was always interspersed with bad times. We would take the baby for long walks and marvel at how quickly he was becoming a little person, but at times Paul would be critical of my mothering. We liked to go out to nice restaurants and we would occasionally leave Alex with a babysitter so we could have a "date night." Looking back now, I realize that most of these dates ending up with us fighting. I thought we were trying to make the relationship work, but there was always tension. I never knew what would set him off.

Paul was less physically abusive after the baby was born, but he was much more emotionally and financially controlling. Paul and I agreed that I would stop working when the baby was born, but now that I didn't bring in a salary, I was completely financially dependent on him. I had to ask him for money for everything . . . including food and diapers. He would yell that I was spending too much, but my spending was never excessive. It was like he had no idea how many diapers a baby needs!

I felt more and more confused. Paul was no longer hitting me, but I felt more stressed and anxious. I contacted a counseling agency for help. They asked lots of questions and then gave me some information about a support group for women who have been abused. At first I was hesitant to go because I didn't think I was experiencing abuse. Sure, Paul was controlling, I thought, but not abusive. I went because I was desperate. Hearing other women's stories was so powerful. I immediately felt that this was a group of women who understood me and all the crazy stuff that was going on with Paul.

Looking back on it, I see now that Paul just got smarter about his abuse. He appeared to be managing his anger by not hitting me, but he increased his control over me in other ways. It was hard for me to consider leaving when I didn't feel physically at risk. It has taken a long time for me to figure out what's normal arguing and what's abuse.

A lot of things kept me from leaving the relationship. I thought I was a failure if I couldn't make it work, and I really wanted a family for Alex and me. I loved my little home and didn't want to leave it, and anytime I suggested I might leave, Paul threatened that he would get custody of Alex and I would end up penniless. I was afraid of upsetting Alex's life and losing everything that mattered to me.

We did eventually separate, but Paul made that very difficult, too. He fought me on custody, access, and support payments.

Once I got some distance from Paul, his abuse continued, but it didn't affect me nearly as much. The ongoing support of my women's group was amazing. My family and close friends saw how Paul treated me and were so relieved that I was not with him. It helped so much that they weren't pressuring me to make the relationship work.

Some of the decisions that I had to make were really hard, and I never had any guarantees that things would work out. I worried about losing custody of Alex and not having a safe home to raise him. But despite Paul's ongoing attempts to undermine and control us, our lives are so much better and happier now. Alex and I are happy in our own little home and neighborhood; the two of us are a family. Not all women need to leave their relationship to feel safe, but I did.

ONE

Am I Experiencing Abuse?

I didn't see myself as an abused woman. The only images I had came from television. I thought of abused women as weak, quiet, and less educated—women who were battered and bruised. That wasn't who I was at all. And my partner certainly didn't fit my image of an abusive husband. I thought they were wild and out of control—men who drank too much, were brutal and hateful. My partner's behavior was confusing. I saw him being kind and pleasant to our friends and family. He was often loving to me, and I loved him. But he got angry so easily; and when he was angry, he was hurtful. Since his hurtful behavior was always directed at me, I believed I was the cause of the abuse.

—MAGGIE

AM I AN "ABUSED WOMAN"?

Was it difficult for you to pick up this book? Is it hard even to consider if you are being abused in your relationship? If it is a struggle even to ask the question, you are not alone. Many women find it hard to imagine that they are being abused by their partners. Part of the struggle has to do with the negative stereotype our culture has of "battered women" and "abusive men." For many people, their description of an abused woman may include: *weak, poor, uneducated, insecure, lacking boundaries,* or *making bad choices.* The truth is, women who are abused by their partners are like any other women. Some are professionals, some are homemakers, some are wealthy, some are living in poverty. Women who experience abuse come from all economic, racial, religious, and ethnic backgrounds.

Similarly, abusive men don't fit neatly into a "type" either. We think of abusive men as monstrous and out of control. We see them as uneducated, not able to hold a job, alcoholic, or a drug addict. But in reality, abusive men may be successful in their jobs, active in their communities, and viewed as upstanding citizens. They can appear to be quite charming and sociable. Friends, family, and neighbors can think abusive men are good people because they are good at hiding the abuse. They may seem to be good fathers. Some abusive men even appear to be progressive in their attitudes about women.

You may have struggled to reconcile your experience of abuse with all these negative stereotypes. If neither you nor your partner fit the stereotype, it may be hard to imagine that you're actually being abused. However, we encourage you to pay attention to your experience rather than to the stereotypes. You will notice as you read this book that we always refer to "women who experience abuse," and not "abused" or "battered women." That is because women are much more than the abuse they experience. You are a person with many qualities and gifts. There is nothing typical about a woman experiencing abuse, except for the abuse itself. Remember: *What you are experiencing has nothing to do with who you are.*

It might be useful for you to identify all the negative descriptions associated with the stereotypes. Take a moment to think about the stereotypes many people hold about abused or "battered" women. Jot them down on the next page.

_____

_____

_____

_____

Would you define yourself in terms of these stereotypes? Of course not. None of us would. Thankfully, not one of them is true. There is only one thing that women who are experiencing abuse have in common: They are being abused by their partners. It sounds straightforward, doesn't it? But it's amazing how many ideas distract us from this basic truth.

Another misconception is that abuse means physical violence. Many women feel that because their partner doesn't hit, push, or in any way physically hurt them, they are not being abused. Abuse takes many forms. You may well be experiencing emotional, physical, financial, or sexual abuse from your partner. This book will help you to know if you are being abused.

If you have picked up this book, you are obviously not comfortable with the dynamics in your relationship or with your partner's behavior. We hope you will find the tools here to help bring clarity to your situation and support your decisions as you move forward.

As I started to read about abuse and attend my support group for women, I had very conflicting emotions. On the one hand, it was good to finally figure out what was really going on in my relationship. On the other hand, I struggled with feeling ashamed that somehow this had happened to me. I was also scared that if I really admitted that I was being abused, I would then have to leave my partner. That was something I really didn't want to do. Looking back on it *now, I realize that those conflicting emotions were only natural, and all I could do was be patient and gentle with myself.*

—SARAH

WHAT'S WRONG IN MY RELATIONSHIP?

You may have asked yourself, "What's wrong in my relationship?" You have probably considered many explanations in order to try to understand the problem. Let's look at some of these explanations.

Most ideas about relationship problems suggest that men and women are equally responsible. Sayings such as "It takes two to tango" reflect this cultural belief. In relationships that are respectful, and when women are not worried about how their partners will respond or behave, we agree that men and women share responsibility for problems in the relationship. There is a problem with the idea of shared responsibility, however, when a man is controlling or abusive. In such cases it is often assumed that the woman has done something to cause the abuse—she has provoked him. In one way or another, women are often held partially responsible for the abuse in their relationship. *In no way are you responsible for the abuse your partner inflicts!* How your partner acts and the choices he makes are his responsibility alone. Nothing that you say or do can justify your partner's abuse.

In our experience, women who are being abused seek many solutions and explanations in order to improve their relationship. You may have gone to counseling by yourself or with your partner, or you may have asked your partner to attend an anger management program (or attended one yourself). Perhaps you have read other self-help books that have suggested that the problem has to do with the natural differences between men and women and that you simply need to accept your partner the way he is. Other books may have implied that you are codependent, love too much, or have problems asserting yourself. Based on suggestions from counselors or self-help books, you have probably tried to change your behavior in order to get your partner to treat you with respect.

If you are experiencing abuse, the problem will persist no matter what you try to change about yourself, your partner, or your relationship. This is because the problem is *his* abuse—his need to have control in your relationship. The sad truth is that you can't change the one thing that really matters—stopping your partner's abuse. Only he can choose to stop being abusive. Until then, everything that takes place in the relationship is related to the abuse. When a man is abusive in his relationship, he alone is responsible for the abuse.

There is nothing you can do to change your partner, but there are things you can do for yourself. This book will help you to understand your situation and it will suggest ways to care for yourself and your children.

WHY WAS I ATTRACTED TO HIM?

Remember when you first met your partner? Did he act in the same abusive ways he does now? When he first met you, did he shake your hand and say, "Hello, my name is Bob and I am abusive. Let's move in together"? Of course not. If he had, you wouldn't have had anything more to do with him! Similarly, if on your first date he'd treated you the way he treats you now, would you have had a second date?

In reflecting back on their relationship, women describe the early period as generally being positive and loving. They didn't observe any abusive behavior until they were committed to the relationship. When women in group counseling list the positive qualities they saw in their partner when they first met him, they always generate a substantial list. Like you, none of these women thought abuse could happen to them.

Sometimes women describe their partner as a hardworking and stable man. Sometimes their partner appears to be a "good family man" in that he seems to be good with children or to value family connections. Sometimes women will reflect on how thoughtful their partner was or that they found their partner easy to talk with or fun to be around.

You may describe different things that attracted you to your partner. Whatever they were, they were positive qualities. Think back to your first experiences of your partner and all the things that attracted you to him. What interested you about him? Remember, you are making a list of the qualities you saw in him when you first met him, not those you see in him now.

_____

_____

_____

_____

Look over the characteristics you thought your partner had. Don't they seem to be attractive and positive? It's important to remind yourself that you were attracted to good things in your partner. You were not attracted to the abuse. The list you made above is a list that anyone, in any relationship, could generate about their partner.

When you first began your relationship, much in it seemed positive to you. If that hadn't been the case, you probably would have ended the relationship before it really began. And, of course, your partner still has some good qualities.[2]

HOW DID I GET HERE?

When you first met your partner, you probably experienced a period of courtship that was enjoyable and that firmly established your relationship. At some point while dating him, however, something may have happened that made you uncomfortable. Perhaps your partner raised his voice, accused you of having an affair, swore at you, argued relentlessly, or threw something.

For some women, the first experience of abuse can be even more subtle. For example, perhaps he was very late for a date and didn't offer an appropriate apology or explanation. Or maybe your partner told mutual friends a private and embarrassing story about you. Remind yourself, however, that regardless of what your partner's first disrespectful or abusive behavior was, it happened within the context of lots of positive things.

You probably overlooked that first instance of bad behavior. You had some good reasons for overlooking it. Your partner may have offered explanations for his behavior or may have apologized to you. Because you are a generous person, you likely accepted his explanation or apology. Perhaps you reminded yourself that no one is perfect

---

2 Sometimes women are abused in more than one of their intimate relationships. If this is true for you, simply focus on one relationship at a time as you work through this book.

and that it is normal for couples to disagree. You may also have reminded yourself of all the good qualities in your partner—the things you appreciated about him. So after some discomfort over his behavior, you tried to let the incident go so that you could feel connected and close to your partner again.

If your partner's poor behavior had been a one-time incident, there would be no problem. But there was a next time and a next time and a next time.

WHAT CAN I DO?

Our goal in writing this book is to offer you an opportunity to make sense of your relationship for yourself. If your partner has imposed his opinions and beliefs on you, you may be left not trusting your own thoughts about the relationship. If he is saying to you, "If you didn't push my buttons, if you weren't so lazy/stupid/bitchy, etc., I wouldn't act this way," you may feel pressured to take responsibility for the problems. Perhaps friends, family, and professionals have offered perspectives like "this is part of a relationship" or "all marriages take work" or "he had a terrible childhood, you need to be more supportive." All this may create further doubt in your mind that you are seeing the relationship problems accurately. You may also feel that your fears and concerns about the relationship are being dismissed. As you read through this book, we hope that you will be able to interpret your relationship and your partner's behavior in a way that reflects your own experiences, thoughts, feelings, and insights. Through this process, you can describe for yourself who you are, what you expect, and what you need from your partner.

You are probably already doing many things to make sense of your situation—meeting your needs and planning your immediate and long-term future. Perhaps you don't realize or appreciate all the mental and emotional work this entails. Reading this book and other books, getting appropriate counseling, resting during a lull in the relationship, making lists, putting money aside, trying to nurture your children and keep them safe—these are all examples of actively looking after yourself. Remember that each of these small steps is extremely important!

Something else you can do at this time is to observe your partner's behavior and compare this with the promises your partner has made to you. We call this work "evidence gathering." It means looking at your partner's behavior as the clearest sign of his intentions. It is giving his actions more weight than his words. For example, if your partner promises to be more truthful with you but continues to lie, you might begin to wonder if what he does is more meaningful than what he says.

While women find the concept of evidence gathering helpful, many also struggle with having to gather evidence about their partner. For some women, it feels wrong to assess their partner's behavior in this way. You have always trusted and been committed to your partner. You've wanted to see the best in him—and you expected that in return. However, in situations of abuse where your partner has hurt you—someone you should feel safe with—he is not fulfilling his commitments to you. He hasn't kept the promises he made at the beginning of the relationship, although these promises have probably kept you hopeful and encouraged about the relationship. Now when he makes promises to change bad behavior, he probably doesn't follow through. As tempting as it is to keep believing in him and his promises, it may be time now to look more closely at what he *does*, rather than what he *says*. We therefore think that focusing on the evidence of his behavior rather than on his promises can help to clarify what's going on in your relationship and help you feel less confused. We hope that the information you gather will help you make the best plans for any future action.

In the next chapter, we will explore some of the evidence in your relationship so that you can begin to understand what is happening to you.

TWO

What Is the Cycle of Abuse?

> My partner's behavior was so crazymaking. It seemed random and out of control. He would blow up over the smallest things. Looking at the Cycle of Abuse helped me start to make sense of my partner's behavior; it had a pattern and a purpose.
>
> —SHEILA

IS THERE A PATTERN?

Most women living with an abusive partner find it hard to see any pattern to the abuse. His behavior seems bizarre and unpredictable. It seems unbelievable that the same person who is kind and affectionate one day could be cruel and malicious another day. His hurtful behavior seems to come as isolated events. You may think of him as a generally "good guy" who does some really awful things once in a while. Or you may be thinking he is abusive, but don't know how to make sense of what is happening.

When we share with women that abuse does have a pattern and a purpose, they begin to see it for themselves. This pattern of behavior is called the Cycle of Abuse.³ There are three distinct phases

---

3 The Cycle was first identified by Lenore Walker in *The Battered Woman* (New York: Harper and Row, Publishers, 1979).

to the Cycle. Below we will review each phase of the Cycle, and describe some of your partner's behaviors.

THE THREE PHASES OF THE CYCLE OF ABUSE

1. Honeymoon phase
2. Tension-building phase
3. Explosion phase

The honeymoon is the first phase of the Cycle of Abuse. For most women, the relationship begins with the *honeymoon phase*, which women often experience as an intense period of courtship. This initial courtship time can last for weeks or months, during which time the relationship is being established. Remember in Chapter 1 when we explored what first attracted you to your partner? This is the honeymoon phase, where your partner's behavior seems positive and he appears to be attentive and considerate. Perhaps he gives you gifts or makes promises, or he may simply behave in a way that seems acceptable or "normal." The two of you begin to build a relationship together. Some women tell us that during this initial phase of the relationship, they worried that it was moving too quickly, but they pushed their concerns down because the relationship seemed positive overall.

The honeymoon is usually followed by a period of *tension building*. This phase of the Cycle will vary in length. Some abusive men may be sullen, silent, unpredictable, or moody for a period of minutes, hours, weeks, or months, leading to unbearable tension in the relationship. At first, your partner's change in behavior may be subtle. Perhaps he makes a sarcastic comment or a hurtful joke at your expense. Perhaps he shows up drunk at your house or pressures you

DIAGRAM 2.1: THE CYCLE OF ABUSE

EXPLOSION

HONEYMOON

TENSION

to have sex. Maybe you don't hear from him for several days, and when he finally contacts you, he claims you have been too "needy" or intense and he needs some space. Up until now, you may not have seen any behaviors that caused you to question your partner and so you may be startled or confused by these changes. You may try to explain his behavior as normal or understandable "ups and downs" in a relationship. As the Cycle continues, your partner's behavior during the tension phase may escalate: He may be outright threatening, angry, or hostile. Perhaps your partner increases his monitoring of your behavior, questioning where you have been and who you have been with. Women often describe their partners as being very critical of them. Some men withdraw from the relationship and appear disinterested and distant. They may justify this behavior with excuses such as stress from work or financial concerns. They may also explain their behavior by blaming their partners or children for creating the problems. Men will often deny that there is a problem, insisting that there is nothing wrong with their behavior. As the Cycle continues, women feel that they are walking on eggshells, living in fear, and trying to avoid an escalation or explosion.

The tension-building phase is followed by the final phase of the Cycle: the *explosion*. The first few incidents of explosion may not feel like a "big deal" to you because it seems like a misunderstanding, disagreement, or argument. You probably didn't think of it as abuse but it didn't feel okay to you either—and it certainly wasn't what you expected. Perhaps your partner raised his voice at you or swore at you. Perhaps he slammed a door or banged a pot down. Perhaps he walked away and gave you the "silent treatment." As your relationship has progressed, you may find that the explosion phase has become worse, marked by increasingly brutal attacks, whether they are physical, verbal, psychological, or sexual. Maybe your partner has cleared out the bank account or accused you of having an affair. Perhaps he has threatened to take the children from you or hurt family or friends. The attacks may also occur more frequently as the relationship progresses. It may feel like living with Dr. Jekyll and Mr. Hyde.

After the explosion, your partner probably returns to the honeymoon phase. Once back in the honeymoon, he stops the negative or dangerous behavior that he demonstrated during the tension-

DIAGRAM 2.2: THE CYCLE OF ABUSE: EXAMPLES OF HIS BEHAVIOR

EXPLOSION
* Intimidating body language
* Constrains me from leaving
* Throws things
* Slams doors
* Silent treatment
* Physical assault
* Name-calling
* Swearing
* Yelling

HONEYMOON
* Apologetic
* Promises to change
* Shows affection
* Wants to have sex
* Agrees to go for counseling
* Shows interest in communicating
* More attentive to family and me
* Helps around the house
* Gives gifts and compliments

TENSION
* Insults
* Threats
* Sarcasm
* Jealousy
* Accusations
* Faultfinding
* Controls what I do
* Quick mood changes
* Emotionally distant

building and explosion phases and shows the side of himself that you were initially attracted to. Your partner may apologize and promise not to act in such an aggressive manner again, or he may simply resume behaving in a way that is acceptable to you. There are many tactics that he may use to convince you to stay with him.

Being a caring, forgiving person, you accept his apology, promises, or changed behavior, and your relationship and the Cycle continue.

In real life, the Cycle might not feel so predictable. You may notice over time that your partner's behavior during the tension-building and explosion phases becomes more extreme. His behavior during the honeymoon phase may also change; he may give more gifts and make more promises in order to "win you back." Alternatively, some women find that the honeymoon period virtually disappears, and the relationship becomes characterized by the tension-building and explosion phases.

Some people think that the explosion phase is where the abuse happens and that when you return to the honeymoon, the abuse has ended and the relationship is "back on track." Now that we have reviewed the Cycle, you may begin to see that your partner's actions in all phases of the Cycle are designed to maintain power and control. *Each of the phases of the Cycle are abusive*, but in different ways and with different effects on you.

On the previous page is a diagram of the Cycle of Abuse. We've added examples from what women share at our support groups. It will give you some ideas of the behaviors that abusive men demonstrate during each of these phases.

Perhaps you would now like to complete a Cycle for yourself. Beginning with the honeymoon phase, describe the behaviors and beliefs that your partner demonstrates that seem positive or that you were initially attracted to. Then list the behaviors your partner demonstrates during the tension-building phase and, finally, the explosion phase.

Women tell us that trying to manage the relationship and avoid the tension-building and explosion phases consumes all their energy and concentration. There is little time to reflect on these patterns.

THE CYCLE OF ABUSE
My Experience of His Behavior

_____

_____

_____

_____

EXPLOSION _____

HONEYMOON

_____

_____

_____

_____

TENSION

_____

_____

_____

_____

_____

We hope that drawing a Cycle for yourself has provided you with an opportunity to identify the patterns in his behavior.

WHEN IS A HONEYMOON NOT A HONEYMOON?

For many women, the honeymoon phase is the most confusing part of the Cycle. Your partner behaves in ways that appear to be loving or remorseful, but you may still feel uncomfortable. This confusion may keep you in your relationship. For example, just as you feel ready to "give up on the relationship," possibly even making plans to leave, your partner changes his behavior or at least promises to do so; you then find yourself hopeful and reengaged in the relationship. During the honeymoon phase, your partner appears to be kind to you, but many women can look back on the honeymoon and feel that they have been manipulated. Let's look at an example.

IRENE

Irene has been unhappy in her marriage for a long time. She has considered leaving her partner, Dean, on several occasions. One night, she and Dean argued for several hours about their financial situation. Dean kept escalating the argument until he was screaming at her and calling her names. Dean's behavior frightened Irene, and she resolved to move out. The next morning, Dean helped get the children off to school (something he never did) and apologized very sincerely for his behavior the previous evening. He admitted that he had a problem with his anger and promised to take an anger management course. Irene is encouraged by his help with the children, his sincere apology, and his promise to seek counseling. She decides to give the relationship one more chance.

The honeymoon phase is confusing because *what appears to be caring behavior is often controlling.* You may find this idea jarring. Let's explore it further. Think about some of the things your partner offers during the honeymoon phase, such as a gift, a promise, an apology, sex, or help with the kids. How do you feel about accepting what he has offered? Although you may feel grateful that the explosion is over, do you sometimes feel unready to accept the peace offering?

Women often feel unable to refuse what is being offered (or forced on them) during the honeymoon phase. They know there will be negative consequences if they decline the offer. When you understand your partner's motives, you can understand that his gestures during the honeymoon phase are still largely about controlling you. While your partner may appear to be genuinely concerned for you, his actions are about staying in control.

Let's think this through in more concrete terms. Are you free to reject his overtures during the honeymoon time without fear of abuse? (We don't suggest you actually do this because it might be dangerous for you. Simply ask yourself if you could.) For example, if he comes home during a honeymoon phase with an expensive gift, are you free not to accept it? Although you may wish he had not spent money on jewelry when there are bills to pay, are you free to say so? If he suggests going on a walk together, are you free to say "no"? Can you tell him you are too tired for a walk without eventual negative consequences?

Imagine this scenario: You and a friend are hosting a dinner party together. After you have arranged to use her house because it is larger, you find out that she's been sick all week. Wanting to help her, you offer to do some of her housecleaning. Being embarrassed by the state of her house, your friend kindly declines your offer.

How do you respond? Can you imagine responding with abuse? Can you imagine telling your friend that she's stupid for not accepting your offer, that she is going to ruin your party, and that you are so insulted you will no longer attend? Of course you wouldn't respond this way, but this may be the way your partner behaves when you don't respond the way he wants during the honeymoon phase.

If you do not feel free to decline your partner's overtures during the honeymoon phase, it says something quite negative about his motives. If something is offered as a "gift" or "kind gesture," you should feel free to accept it or not. If your partner doesn't give you that choice, clearly he is focusing on his need to stay in control rather than on your well-being. If you don't go along with the honeymoon, he may become aggressive or hurtful. Some abusive men also become sulky or accuse their partners of being "unwilling to work on the relationship." These behaviors are different forms of abuse, which we will examine more closely in Chapter 4.

Your partner's actions during the honeymoon stage certainly look sincere, but over time you begin to experience them differently. He is behaving as he does in order to have things his way, not out of a real interest in caring for you or in nurturing the relationship. His "kindness" is actually very manipulative. This may be a painful realization for you. Even when he seems to be loving and caring, it's actually about controlling you. The following are two stories to illustrate this point.

> *My partner gave me a new cell phone. I didn't even want the phone but I couldn't tell him I didn't want it. It would have made him mad. Now I can't even go to the grocery store without him calling*

to ask what I'm doing. I really have to think before I make a call because he gets the bill. For "my safety" he insists I carry it all the time. If I leave it behind, he says I am forgetful and don't appreciate his gift.

—JANINE

I have a chronic illness and it means a lot of medical appointments. My partner insists on coming with me to see my doctor. At first it seemed like he was concerned about my health and cared about me. But now it feels like he kind of takes over the appointment and I feel like the doctor listens to him more than me.

—AUDREY

The honeymoon phase leaves a woman feeling confused precisely because it is confusing. She might be resolved to leave after an explosion. But her partner returns the relationship to the honeymoon, and she may feel guilty about leaving. It looks like he is trying. He may be promising to go for help or "do anything" to save the relationship. Women feel obligated to stick around and "give him one more chance." Some aspects of the honeymoon keep women feeling hopeful while at other times they simply feel trapped.

The honeymoon phase keeps you working on the relationship. If the relationship consisted only of tension-building and explosion, you may not continue to be hopeful. However, your partner is not always explosive; sometimes his behavior seems acceptable and you feel attracted to him. Your partner seems sincere in what he says during the honeymoon phase, and you want to believe him. Because his behavior during the honeymoon phase seems positive and because you hope that this time the change will be genuine and permanent, you stay in the relationship. For this reason, some women describe the honeymoon as a period of entrapment—the hope your partner creates is the hook that keeps you in the relationship. Other people refer to the honeymoon phase as manipulative kindness, because that is what it is. It is certainly not a honeymoon in the usual sense of the word.

Some women don't experience much honeymoon behavior. All they get from their partner is a pattern of tension and explosion. In our experience, this happens when women are really trapped and so their partners don't need to do anything positive to keep the woman in the relationship. For example, women may be trapped because they have small children and no income, live in a rural or remote area, have health concerns, or have all their savings tied up in his business. Whatever her circumstances, her partner no longer needs to hook her back into the relationship. She is stuck.

We realize that looking at the honeymoon phase as a negative and harmful part of the relationship may be difficult for you to hear. Perhaps it has been the one part of the relationship that you have held on to as your hope for future change—and when you have felt safer and more independent. It is our hope that as you continue to read, you will find hope in the new understanding that you are gaining.

WHO IS IN CONTROL OF THE CYCLE?

The Cycle of Abuse is your partner's cycle. He is in control of it. Through it, he uses a variety of tactics to achieve his goal of maintaining power over you. You may not have thought of his behavior in this way before—perhaps it has always seemed random to you.

Maybe you've described his behavior as out of control rather than a means of maintaining control.

Some women believe that they are responsible for the Cycle or that they cause the abuse. Your partner may even have suggested this. He will tell you that he lost his temper only because you were "pushing his buttons." Women may also feel that they are driving the Cycle because some of their own behavior looks explosive or controlling.

Sometimes there is a period of escalation before the explosion. It is not uncommon for a woman to yell, swear, throw something, or even hit her partner during this very tense period. This happens in response to his ongoing, oppressive behaviors. In our experience, women behaving in this way are most often attempting to protect themselves or to end the tension-building phase. If your partner has been increasing the tension for days or is building it to a level that is no longer tolerable for you, you may do something to break the tension-building phase, knowing that there will be an explosion followed by the relief of the honeymoon. You may or may not be aware of doing this. Regardless, we know that you are just trying to stop the crazy and unrelenting attacks on your emotional and physical well-being, and that you are not trying to control or frighten your partner. Be reassured that you are having a normal response to a very difficult situation.

I remember thinking that my partner seemed determined to pick a fight, so we might as well get it over with. I would then stand up for myself in a given argument, and the explosion would inevitably come. During the first several years of our marriage, I occasionally yelled, swore, or threw something at my partner. Once, after three hours of

*unrelenting emotional attacks, I slammed down an iron and broke
it. All of this behavior concerned me. It was not the way I wanted
to be in my relationship. Now that my partner is no longer abusive,
I no longer do the things that disturbed me.*

—SANDI

Although you may have behaved in ways that are unacceptable
to you, it is important to emphasize that your partner is the one
who controls the Cycle of Abuse. The explosion will inevitably come.
No matter what you do, your partner will find some reason to be
abusive. He will attempt to use your behavior to justify his explosion,
but nothing you do justifies his abuse. He will equate your "bad"
behavior with his, but they are not equal. Your motives are not the
same. He is attempting to regain control and is using threatening
and abusive tactics to do that. You are protecting your physical and
mental well-being and attempting to be heard or to have some say
in your relationship. You've tried many different things to fix the
relationship and stop his controlling behavior. But no matter what
you do or how hard you try, you keep getting hurt. You cannot
improve the situation because he is 100 percent responsible for the
problem—and the problem is his abuse.

IS THE CYCLE THE SAME FOR EVERYONE?

Hopefully you are connecting on some level with our description
of the Cycle of Abuse. For some women, it rings true the first time
they encounter it. Other women need to explore the Cycle a bit and
perhaps even modify it to better reflect their experiences. The Cycle
may not be as tidy and predictable in real life as it is typed out on
a piece of paper. It may not move predictably from one phase to the

other. The phases may blur together, and they may not follow each other in order. Your partner may jump from phase to phase or linger a long time in one of them. Some women report that, over time, the honeymoon phase is skipped altogether.

For myself, I needed to put the emphasis on the different kinds of behavior my partner demonstrated rather than on the Cycle itself. I wasn't aware so much of us moving in a Cycle as I was of my partner demonstrating three different kinds of behavior. He certainly demonstrated honeymoon behavior, tension-building behavior, and explosion behavior. Sometimes, however, he moved the Cycle directly from honeymoon to explosion, and sometimes he moved it from explosion back to tension building without a honeymoon period. For these reasons, I found it helpful to draw out a Cycle of Abuse that described my own experience.

I imagined the Cycle as a combination padlock, because it illustrated clearly who was at the center of the Cycle and who was controlling it. My partner was the dial on the padlock. He was in the center and the controlling force of the Cycle. He chose where we would be on the Cycle and what behavior he would use to achieve his goal of staying in control. The padlock also helped me realize that the Cycle wouldn't necessarily move from honeymoon to tension building to explosion; it might jump backward or skip a phase.

—EMMA

Each phase of the Cycle is a different expression of power and control, and you are left constantly trying to anticipate what is coming next. The honeymoon phase is often the most confusing because you see the man you were first attracted to and it rekindles hope in you. The tension-building phase of the Cycle of Abuse is different. There is a constant fear that, at any time, your partner could become explosive. Living with the anticipation of the abuse intensifying is extremely exhausting and frightening. The explosion can be very unsafe for women, and may be a time that you consider having to leave. All of this is to say that what you are going through is very hard and you are living under tremendous strain.

We hope the Cycle will give you a different lens through which to view your relationship. If you have been feeling shame about how your partner treats you, hopefully the Cycle makes it clear that you are not to blame and you are not responsible. It gives you a different way to view your partner's behavior and your response. Some women tell us that knowing about the Cycle helps them to step back emotionally from what he is doing and see it more clearly as *his* problem. Always keep in mind, though, that your safety is the number one concern. It may only be when you get a moment to yourself that you can think about your partner's behavior through this lens.

In the next chapter, we will focus on your experiences during the Cycle of Abuse. This focus may help you appreciate more fully the complex and difficult situation you are in.

THREE

How Do I Experience the Cycle of Abuse?

In subtle ways, he tried to control my actions and my thoughts. He always had to prove that he was right and that I was wrong; we couldn't simply disagree. His rage would silence me. I constantly had to decide whether an issue was worth raising with him—if it was safe to bring it up. If he did any housework, he became angry and resentful. He was always picking fights and it was hard to avoid explosive situations. I was exhausted living with him. As time went on, John seemed angry more and more. Finally, when John broke my rib, I began to see the seriousness of our situation. I wondered if this was abuse.

—LORENA

WHY DO I FEEL SO CONFUSED?

In this chapter, we will explore the Cycle of Abuse as you experience it. In the last chapter, we looked at your partner's behavior in each phase of the Cycle, but it is also important to understand how the Cycle and the abuse have affected you. Throughout the Cycle you experience many different reactions and emotions in response to your partner's behaviors. Some of the reactions seem quite contradictory to each other. You may find yourself feeling love and hate, anger and affection, fear and intimacy. It is distressing to live with such a range of emotional reactions, but it is normal to have these feelings.

As well as leaving you exhausted and off balance, your partner's constantly changing behavior also affects how you feel about yourself and how you view yourself. All of us count on the people around us to reflect a realistic picture of who we are. With your partner, you are getting a distorted picture that is constantly changing—and often very negative and damaging. If during the explosion phase, you are told that you are stupid, fat, and ugly but then during the honeymoon phase you are told you are attractive, sexy, and fun to be around, it is difficult to get an accurate picture of yourself and hold on to it.

While your partner is at the center of it and controls it, the Cycle has a profound effect on you. Let's reflect on your experience of each phase of the Cycle.

WHY DOES THE HONEYMOON PHASE MAKE ME FEEL CRAZY?

As you may have already concluded from the previous chapter, the honeymoon phase can be the most difficult phase to figure out. Women can have different kinds of reactions, which, at first glance, may seem rather distinct from each other.

Women are often most hopeful during the honeymoon phase, especially early in their relationship. Being hopeful makes a lot of sense. Your partner is doing something positive. Maybe he's apologized for his explosive behavior; or he's promised never to behave that way again; or he's being considerate (e.g., encouraging you to spend more time with friends); or he's agreed to go for counseling. During this phase of the Cycle, you may do enjoyable things together (e.g., enjoy conversation, have sex, go on family outings). This may be a time when you can let down your guard and recover from the explosion. These positive experiences may make you feel reconnected to your partner and encourage you to think that your relationship is on the mend. This makes sense—your partner's behavior during this phase is intended to create hope in you so that you will stay in the relationship.

Some women, after experiencing the Cycle—perhaps hundreds of times—begin to question the sincerity of the honeymoon phase. If your partner apologizes for swearing at you and then does so in the very next argument, you will begin to doubt the genuineness of his apology. Similarly, if he promises to go for counseling but never manages to make an appointment, you may begin to doubt his promises. Based on this evidence, you may begin to feel skeptical during the honeymoon phase. Women sometimes feel guilty that they don't trust their partner's intentions during the honeymoon phase. We think this skepticism reflects your wisdom. Your experience gives you plenty of evidence to wonder whether he will keep his promises. While you still might be hopeful, you are also allowing yourself to pay attention to the evidence he is presenting to you. It may be very painful for you to be skeptical about someone you love.

As we discussed in Chapter 2, the honeymoon phase can also feel entrapping for women. The honeymoon phase keeps you committed to the relationship. It also serves to control you. You may not feel free to reject your partner's overtures during the honeymoon phase. You might feel coerced into going along with him, even if you disagree. For example, if your partner wants to have sex during this phase, you may not feel free to say "no." If you do, he may become angry or sulky, or he may also accuse you of being cold and distant.

Many women express fear of doing or saying anything that will "set off" their partners and ruin the relative peace of the honeymoon phase. Feeling forced to go along with the honeymoon wears on a woman's well-being. Women feel that they are not being true to themselves as they are pressured to go along with their partner's ideas of what is needed to set things right.

Given the multitude of emotions that you may be feeling, it makes sense for you to have a range of reactions during the honeymoon phase. It makes sense to feel hopeful, skeptical, trapped, resentful, or fearful. Your partner is doing things that can make you feel any or all of these things. It also makes sense if some days you feel skeptical and some days you feel hopeful and some days you feel trapped. The honeymoon phase is really crazy making!

Below is a list of things women have experienced during the honeymoon phase of the Cycle. See if some of these experiences seem familiar to you.

During the Honeymoon Phase, I . . .

- ○ Feel like things are going well.
- ○ Feel safe and secure.
- ○ Feel generous.
- ○ Feel loved and appreciated.
- ○ Feel relaxed.
- ○ Can ask for things.
- ○ Feel like I can express myself.
- ○ Think the relationship is not so bad.
- ○ Feel hopeful.
- ○ Feel positive.
- ○ Feel grateful.
- ○ Enjoy my partner's attention.
- ○ Feel loving and want to be intimate.
- ○ Feel sorry for him.
- ○ Feel energetic.
- ○ Feel free to see friends.
- ○ Feel safe to ask him to do things.

- ○ Feel like I should try harder.
- ○ Feel guilty.
- ○ Feel confused.
- ○ Feel skeptical.
- ○ Become introspective.
- ○ Question the relationship.
- ○ Know he is not being genuine.
- ○ Wonder how long it will last.
- ○ Feel doubtful.
- ○ Feel uncomfortable.
- ○ Feel fake.
- ○ Feel dead/numb.
- ○ Feel distant.
- ○ Feel repelled by his approaches.
- ○ Want to escape.
- ○ _____
- ○ _____
- ○ _____

The honeymoon phase tends to be a time of conflicting emotions and thoughts, leaving you uncertain and confused.

WHY DO I FEEL LIKE I'M WALKING ON EGGSHELLS?

Now ask yourself what happens to you during the tension phase of the Cycle? Many women feel like they are "walking on eggshells" or "through a minefield," never knowing what will set their partner off. Your partner seems angry, hostile, or stressed out. For your safety, you do whatever you can to keep things from getting worse. You may try to be very accommodating during this phase, making everything at home positive and calm. If you have children, you may have learned to keep them quiet or out of sight. You may attempt to respond to all your partner's requests or demands, but no matter what you do, he continues to be demanding, sarcastic, critical, threatening, or sullen.

During this tension phase, you may also begin to feel frustrated. It may feel that no matter what you do, he maintains a high level of tension. He may keep trying to pick fights. Perhaps you feel that he is hypercritical of everything you do—it feels as if you can't do anything without his judgment.

The crazy-making part of the tension phase is that your partner will constantly change the rules. For example, maybe he gets angry when you disagree with him about something. In the hopes of trying to keep things calm, you decide to keep your opinions to yourself. Then he tells you that you are infuriating him because you will not speak your mind. Changing the rules keeps your partner in charge and keeps you desperately trying to figure out how to behave, what to say, what to wear, and even where to look. You may find yourself always second-guessing your own decisions. For example, the first time you wore a new dress, he told you how beautiful you looked, but the next time you wore that dress, he accused you of looking like a whore and having an affair. So how do you decide whether or not to wear that dress again? Women who have experienced abuse describe an endless number of examples similar to this, saying that there is no way to anticipate their partner's response or make a decision that will keep them safe. They feel that they can't do anything right and live in constant fear of taking a step that will lead to the next explosion.

Often women notice physical problems as a result of living with the fear and uncertainty. The extreme stress you are under may lead to health concerns such as headaches, heart palpitations, dizziness, exhaustion, or insomnia. Some women also feel depressed or anxious during this period of the Cycle. Here's how one woman described her experience:

> I would make sure the house was in perfect order before my husband came home from work. This was always a challenge because I ran a daycare out of my home. No matter how hard I worked to make everything look nice, he would always find something to get angry about. I began to be scared day after day, dreading his arrival home from work. I felt very emotional. My blood pressure went up. The kids began to pick up on my fear. I could see they were anxious about their dad coming home, too. I doubted myself and blamed myself. I kept wondering what I could do to change the situation. I now understand it was not me who had to change.
>
> —JANE

To reflect on what is happening for you during this phase of the Cycle, it might be helpful to think of one situation in which you were aware of the tension your partner was creating. Then think about what you experienced during that time, both physically and emotionally. The following are some examples of things that women describe about their experience during the tension phase of the Cycle. Look down the list and see if you have had any of these experiences.

During the Tension Phase, I . . .

○ Try to keep the peace.
○ Keep busy.
○ Keep the kids quiet.
○ Cover up for the kids.
○ Become forgetful.
○ Have problems focusing.
○ Worry.
○ Feel fearful.
○ Second-guess myself.
○ Wonder if I should leave.
○ Think I've made a big mistake.
○ Make lists to try to keep track of everything.
○ Feel like a fool.
○ Feel resigned to the situation.
○ Feel hurt.
○ Feel isolated.
○ Feel exhausted.

○ Feel irritated.
○ Feel angry.
○ Cry a lot.
○ Have a knot in my stomach.
○ Have pains in my chest.
○ Have anxiety attacks.
○ Feel depressed.
○ Have nightmares.
○ Have blurred vision.
○ Over eat/under eat.
○ Can't sleep/sleep too much.
○ Retreat into myself.
○ Think about death as a way to escape.
○ Feel like I can't make a decision.
○ _____
○ _____
○ _____

As you can see from the list, living with constant tension has a devastating effect on your health and well-being as well as on your ability to make decisions that will help keep you safe.

WHY IS THE EXPLOSION SO AWFUL?

Now let's think about what happens to you during the explosion phase of the Cycle. For many women, this is the most dangerous and frightening time in the Cycle. Although men are not out of control, they may appear to be out of control and that is alarming. If your partner is driving recklessly, throwing something in your direction, startling you out of sleep, humiliating you with words, or attacking you physically or sexually, your well-being as a person is being seriously threatened.

As well as being frightened during this phase, women also find the explosion affects their self-identity. The explosions can humiliate and degrade you. If you are told that you are "stupid" or "selfish" or "bitchy," this will obviously undermine your sense of self-worth. It is difficult to feel positive or realistic about yourself when your character is being attacked.

One of the very destructive aspects of the explosion phase is that you are being blamed for the explosion. This can also affect your self-identity and your sense of reality. Let's use an example to illustrate this.

EMILY

Emily, who is married and has two children, is invited by her fellow employees to join them for drinks after work one night. She decides she would like to go. After carefully considering when it would be best to raise this with her partner, she asks him the night before. Emily asks if he could be home from work in time to relieve the babysitter so Emily can go out. She also asks him to make the kids dinner and to watch them until she gets home. He chooses to explode in response to her request. He tells her that she's being self-centered. He reminds her that he has been working hard lately, and the last thing he needs is to come home to babysit the kids. Besides, doesn't she think her kids deserve a piece of her, too? After all, they are stuck with a sitter all day. He also accuses her of being interested in one of her colleagues and suggests that she may be having an affair. Emily is being falsely accused by her partner. Because she is interested in making her marriage work, however, she tries to sort through each of his accusations to see if they hold any truth. She wonders, "Am I being selfish? Have I not paid enough attention to the stress my partner is living with? Am I not giving my kids enough time? Am I being flirtatious at work?"

Constantly having to evaluate herself forces a woman to keep the focus of the problem on her rather than on her partner's controlling and abusive behavior. The result is that women end up trying to make changes to themselves as a way of stopping their partner's abuse.

But no matter how much of the blame or responsibility you have accepted and how much you have sought solutions, your partner continues the Cycle of Abuse. *The abuse is not your fault.* He is responsible for driving the Cycle. You cannot stop the abuse. Below is a list of things women have experienced during the explosion phase of the Cycle. See if anything seems familiar to you.

During the Explosion Phase, I . . .

○ Feel scared.　　　　　　 ○ Feel hopeless.
○ Try to get away.　　　　　○ Feel degraded.
○ Feel trapped.　　　　　　 ○ Become very quiet.

○ Avoid eye contact.   ○ Hit him.
○ Shake.   ○ Hit myself.
○ Give in to him.   ○ Throw things.
○ Try to end the relationship. ○ Shut myself off.
○ Try to protect myself.   ○ Experience physical injuries.
○ Fight back.   ○ _____
○ Yell.   ○ _____
○ Feel like I'm going crazy.   ○ _____
○ Swear.

The explosion phase can be dangerous for you and your children. It is a time of high stress because of the fear you feel. This affects you both physically and psychologically. As a society, we tend to associate the explosion with physical injury and that is sometimes the case. However, women are inevitably harmed psychologically by the explosion phase and that harm is often invisible and long-lasting. These are only some of the ways you may be affected by your partner's explosions.

WHAT IS MY EXPERIENCE OF THE CYCLE?

In our group counseling with women, we sketch out the Cycle of Abuse first from the perspective of the man's behavior (as we did in Chapter 2). Then we sketch out the Cycle from the point of view of the woman's experience. Drawing on all the experiences of the women in the room, we come up with a Cycle that looks something like the one on the next page. When you look at this Cycle, do not be concerned if some of your experience is not represented here; this is only an example.

Looking at the Cycle as a whole, you can appreciate how confusing and complex it really is. Although everything that occurs in

DIAGRAM 3.1: WOMEN'S EXPERIENCE OF THE CYCLE OF ABUSE

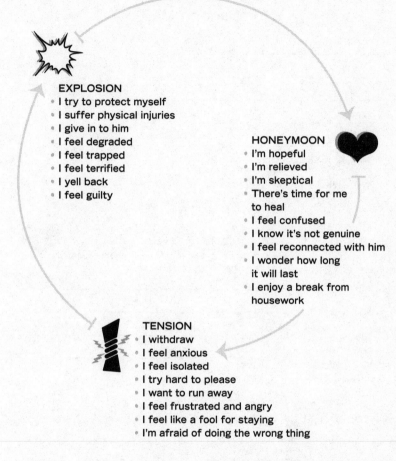

EXPLOSION
- I try to protect myself
- I suffer physical injuries
- I give in to him
- I feel degraded
- I feel trapped
- I feel terrified
- I yell back
- I feel guilty

HONEYMOON
- I'm hopeful
- I'm relieved
- I'm skeptical
- There's time for me to heal
- I feel confused
- I know it's not genuine
- I feel reconnected with him
- I wonder how long it will last
- I enjoy a break from housework

TENSION
- I withdraw
- I feel anxious
- I feel isolated
- I try hard to please
- I want to run away
- I feel frustrated and angry
- I feel like a fool for staying
- I'm afraid of doing the wrong thing

the Cycle is part of the abuse, women tend to experience a wide range of emotions and reactions as their partners are abusive in very different ways throughout the Cycle.

You might want to see what the Cycle looks like for you by putting examples of things you have experienced in the Cycle on the next page. You can take some examples from the lists in this

THE CYCLE OF ABUSE
Impact on Me

_____

_____

_____

_____

✳ EXPLOSION _____

♥ HONEYMOON

_____

_____

_____

_____

TENSION _____

_____

_____

_____

_____

_____

chapter and put them in the appropriate phases. This might help you to create a picture of what's going on for you as your partner continues to control you and your relationship through the Cycle of Abuse.

The Cycle affects each woman differently. Hopefully you are beginning to see for yourself how your partner's abusive behavior during each phase of the Cycle affects you and how the Cycle overall impacts you in a very negative way.

You may have many reactions to what you have read in this chapter. Looking at the Cycle you've created may be overwhelming, liberating, or both. Up until this point, you have not been able to pay much attention to yourself or the larger pattern of the relationship. You have been forced to put all your attention on your partner in hopes of diminishing or stopping the abuse. Focusing on his immediate needs, moods, and demands may not give you the opportunity to see how his abuse is affecting you.

It may make you very sad, or angry, or frightened to realize that there is a pattern to the abuse you've experienced and that the abuse takes so many forms. It may also be very liberating, especially if you have felt that you are "going crazy" because your emotions or life seem out of control. Hopefully, you are beginning to see that you are not crazy, but your partner's behavior is certainly crazy making. We will look more closely at the effect your partner's abuse is having on you in Chapter 5. Now let's turn our attention to the different kinds of abuse you may be experiencing.

FOUR

What Are the Different Types of Abuse?

I remember him being angry. He pulled all my clothes out of the closet and threw them on the floor. Then he pulled out all the drawers from my dresser. The whole time he kept yelling at me and telling me I was stupid. I was so overwhelmed and frightened, I went into our spare room and just cried. He came in and tried to console me. I was so hurt, angry, and humiliated—I just kept crying. In the morning I cleaned up the mess. I wondered what my little girl thought. I didn't say anything to him for fear of making him mad again. He acted like it had never happened, so I had to do the same. And life went on.

—JEN

HOW DO I EXPERIENCE ABUSE?

Abuse takes many forms. Some people may believe that if women are not being physically hurt, it is not really that "bad." Maybe you have had the same thought. We have learned from women that no one type of abuse is worse than another type. All abuse has a negative impact on you. The Cycle of Abuse demonstrates that abuse is not just hitting; it's not just being called names, or having things thrown at you. It's financial; it's sexual; it's spiritual. It's using the children to manipulate you, and many other things. The abuse that is the most subtle or manipulative can be the most difficult to identify and may make you think the problem is yours: "You're too sensitive," "you're jealous," "you're crazy," etc. When your abusive partner is so charming to others and everyone seems to like him, you may wonder if what is happening to you is even real or if you are imagining things.

Despite women's experiences, many people think that physical abuse is the worst type and some believe it is the only type of abuse. What we hear from women who are abused is that emotional, psychological, and verbal abuse are extremely damaging forms of abuse and can affect women for a long time. These forms of abuse can be difficult to identify and name. They also tend to be more pervasive in our society and thus may be more "hidden." Some people might even think of them as fights or disagreements without understanding the context of power and control. Maybe you have wondered if you are expecting too much of your partner or that conflict is just part of the normal ups and downs of a relationship. These are some of the messages women hear from others: "My mother says disagreements are part of marriages," "my friend says I'm too sensitive and he didn't mean anything by it," "my brother says I'm not perfect either," or "my counselor says that I'm just playing the victim." What are some of the messages you have heard that have kept you from naming your reality accurately?

No one but you can assess how your partner's abuse has affected you or what types of abuse are most painful. We will further explore the effects of the abuse in Chapter 5. For now, let's look at the many ways that women experience abuse from their intimate partners.

EMOTIONAL ABUSE

USING CULTURE

Using his culture as an excuse for abuse, Putting down my culture, Forcing me to adopt his cultural practices, Not allowing me to participate in mainstream culture

Teasing, Invalidating feelings, Using guilt, Blaming me for everything, Being jealous, Threatening, Withholding affection, Waking me up, Silent treatment, Stalking

SOCIAL ABUSE

Isolating me from my friends and family, Monitoring phone calls or mileage, Dictating who I can see, Preventing me from working

POWER &

USING CHILDREN

Abusing children, Threatening to harm or take children away, Refusing to make support payments, Belittling me in front of children, Using visitation as leverage

Putting down my faith, Cutting me off from my church, Using church and faith to his advantage, Soul-destroying behavior, Using scripture against me

Threatening to or having an affair, Forcing or manipulating sex, Sexual put-downs, Criticizing how I dress, Withholding sex, Comparing me to others, Using pornography, Demanding sex as payment

SPIRITUAL ABUSE

SEXUAL ABUSE

INTELLECTUAL ABUSE

Making me prove things to him, Mind games, Demanding perfection, Making me feel stupid, Attacking my ideas and opinions, Manipulation of information, Telling me I'm crazy

FINANCIAL ABUSE

Calling welfare, Limiting access to money, Making me account for every penny, Controlling the money, Closing bank accounts, Wasting, Creating debt, Not paying child support, Taking care of own needs

PETS & PROPERTY ABUSE

Killing or threatening pets, Punching walls and doors, Throwing things, Damaging vehicles, Smashing and breaking things

PSYCHOLOGICAL ABUSE

Intimidating gestures or actions, Threatening suicide, Threatening to kill me, Displaying weapons, Denying he said things, Making light of the abuse

Blocking exits, Driving too fast, Locking me out of the house, Intimidating me, Punching or kicking me, Spitting on me, Choking me, Hitting me, Restraining me

PHYSICAL ABUSE

Name-calling, Swearing, Yelling at me, Insulting me, Being condescending, Being sarcastic

VERBAL ABUSE

CONTROL

WHAT IS THE POWER AND CONTROL WHEEL?

In order to examine the types of abuse, we will use something called the Power and Control Wheel.[4] The Wheel is divided into twelve sections that represent the different types of abuse (e.g., financial, verbal, emotional, etc.). Within each section of the Wheel, we list examples of control that your partner might use. We call these the "tactics" of abuse. You will notice that at the center of the Wheel is written "Power & Control." This indicates that all tactics of abuse are intended to maintain power and control in the relationship. No matter what tactics your partner uses, the effect is to control and intimidate you or to make you feel that you do not have an equal voice in the relationship.

WHAT ARE THE TYPES OF ABUSE?

It is difficult with one small Power and Control Wheel to list all the different tactics of abuse within each section of the Wheel. A more complete list that summarizes many women's experiences is provided on the next page, beginning with a brief description of the type of abuse.

We invite you to look over these lists and check off any kind of abuse you feel you have experienced. You may find that you check off more examples of abuse in one category than another. You may also find that you do not check off anything in some categories. You may want to add to this list from your own experience. Each woman's experience is unique.

---

4 The Power and Control Wheel was originally developed by the Domestic Abuse Intervention Project in Duluth, Minnesota. Our Wheel is adapted from the original with permission.

Psychological/Mental Abuse
Any act intended to undermine your mental well-being and make you feel crazy.

- ○ Telling me I'm crazy
- ○ Giving me the silent treatment
- ○ Manipulating me
- ○ Playing mind games
- ○ Wearing down my instincts
- ○ Watching or monitoring me
- ○ Stalking me
- ○ Distorting reality
- ○ Bringing up the past to deflect the issue at hand
- ○ Using information against me
- ○ Rewriting/distorting history
- ○ Intimidating or threatening me and claiming he's "just joking"
- ○ Putting on a good show to win others to his side
- ○ Giving me glaring looks
- ○ Making me prove things to him
- ○ Demanding perfection
- ○ Changing the rules
- ○ _____
- ○ _____
- ○ _____

Physical/Threat of Physical Abuse
Any unwanted physical contact or threat of physical harm.

- ○ Making threatening gestures
- ○ Driving recklessly
- ○ Throwing things at me or near me
- ○ Restraining me
- ○ Blocking my exit from the room
- ○ Pushing, shoving, hitting, slapping, or punching
- ○ Using weapons to threaten me or the children
- ○ Spitting
- ○ Choking
- ○ Pulling my hair
- ○ Biting or pinching
- ○ Kicking
- ○ Grabbing or shaking
- ○ Locking me out of the house
- ○ Threatening to kill me
- ○ _____
- ○ _____
- ○ _____

Verbal Abuse

Any use of words or volume of voice
to threaten, belittle, or hurt you.

○ Yelling or screaming

○ Putting me down

○ Swearing

○ Using sarcasm and hurtful
"jokes"

○ Saying "you always . . ." or
"you never . . ."

○ Blaming me

○ Being condescending

○ Silent treatment

○ Name-calling

○ Making verbal threats

○ _____

○ _____

○ _____

Sexual Abuse

Any unwanted sexual contact or using
sexuality to hurt or control you.

○ Ridiculing me for saying "no"

○ Forcing sexual acts that I do
not consent to

○ Withholding sex because he
says I'm undesirable

○ Using my past sexual
experience against me

○ Insisting on using
pornography

○ Having or threatening to have
an affair

○ Coercing sex by guilt,
harassment, or threats

○ Forcing sex (rape)

○ Criticizing how I dress (too
sexy or not sexy enough)

○ Telling me I'm not "good
enough"

○ Telling me I'm fat and
undesirable

○ Putting me down sexually
(e.g., calling me whore, slut,
frigid, prude, etc.)

○ Demanding sex as payment

○ Talking to others about our
sex life

○ _____

○ _____

○ _____

Spiritual Abuse

Any word or action that damages you spiritually.

○ Using scripture against me

○ Turning the leaders of my faith against me

○ Turning my faith community against me

○ Attacking my beliefs

○ Preventing me from practicing my faith

○ Preventing my children from learning about my faith

○ Isolating me from my faith community

○ Criticizing or belittling my faith

○ Making me feel rejected or unworthy

○ Forcing me to adopt his beliefs

○ _____

○ _____

○ _____

Using Children

Any involvement, manipulation, threats,
or use of children in the abuse.

○ Belittling me in front of the children

○ Using the children to his advantage

○ Threatening to take the children from me

○ Fighting me for custody of the children

○ Not paying child support

○ Telling me I'm a terrible mother

○ Telling the children I'm a terrible mother

○ Lying to the children

○ Lying to the children about me

○ Threatening to harm the children

○ Harming the children

○ Using visitation to harass me

○ _____

○ _____

○ _____

Social Abuse

Any attempt to isolate you or cut you off from
sources of support and care.

○ Restricting where I go and
what I do

○ Cutting me off from friends
and family

○ Embarrassing me in front of
others

○ Controlling who I spend
time with

○ Refusing to spend time with
my family

○ Being jealous

○ Criticizing family members
and friends so I stop
seeing them

○ Monitoring my phone calls

○ Reading my e-mails

○ Controlling my Facebook
account

○ Checking my cell phone
record

○ Demanding explanations for
my interactions with others

○ Monitoring car mileage

○ Preventing me from working

○ Preventing me from moving
forward in my work

○ Preventing me from going to
school

○ _____

○ _____

○ _____

Using Culture

Any use of cultural ideas as a way to
dominate or belittle you.

○ Using culture to legitimize
abusive behavior

○ Putting down my culture

○ Forcing me to adopt his
cultural practices

○ Speaking his language to
exclude me

○ Using extended family to
oppress or abuse me

○ Refusing to allow me to learn
mainstream culture or
language

○ _____

○ _____

○ _____

Emotional Abuse

Any act intended to undermine your emotional well-being
or cause emotional harm or confusion.

○ Teasing
○ Trying to tell me how to feel
○ Putting me in a "no-win" situation
○ Using a threatening tone of voice
○ Being jealous
○ Intimidating me
○ Changing mood quickly (e.g., from calm to anger)
○ Giving mixed messages (e.g., love and hate)
○ Behaving unpredictably

○ Withdrawing emotionally
○ Making me feel guilty
○ Being competitive
○ Invalidating my feelings
○ Blaming me for everything
○ Withholding affection
○ Waking me up in the middle of the night
○ Threatening suicide
○ Making light of the abuse
○ _____
○ _____
○ _____

Intellectual Abuse

Any act intended to make you doubt your intellectual
ability and make you feel inferior.

○ Making me look stupid
○ Claiming superior intelligence
○ Correcting my grammar
○ Correcting me in front of others
○ Devaluing my opinions or knowledge
○ Confusing me
○ Belittling my intellectual ability

○ Not letting me finish my sentences
○ Showing off his higher education
○ Belittling my education or career
○ _____
○ _____
○ _____

Financial Abuse
Any intentional act that deprives you (or your children)
of financial security or limits your access
to financial decision making.

- ○ Making me account for every dollar
- ○ Making me justify every purchase
- ○ Withholding financial information
- ○ Hiding money from me
- ○ Limiting my access to money
- ○ Closing out joint bank accounts without my consent
- ○ Spending money needed for the household on himself (or gambling it away)
- ○ Making major purchases or transactions without my consent
- ○ Belittling my financial contributions to the household

- ○ Threatening to take all the money if I should separate
- ○ Refusing to pay for child-related expenses
- ○ Spending money carelessly
- ○ Making me beg for money
- ○ Forcing me to commit welfare fraud
- ○ Running up bills
- ○ Leaving me with the burden of paying bills when there's not enough money
- ○ Making financial decisions without me
- ○ Not paying child support
- ○ _____
- ○ _____
- ○ _____

Abuse of Pets and Property
Hurting pets or damaging property in order
to intimidate, control, and hurt you.

- ○ Threatening to hurt pets
- ○ Neglecting or killing pets
- ○ Punching walls and doors
- ○ Throwing things
- ○ Damaging the car

- ○ Smashing things
- ○ Breaking treasured items
- ○ _____
- ○ _____
- ○ _____

WHAT IS HIS MOTIVE?

It's important here to say a word about your partner's motives. As you looked over these lists, you may have discovered behaviors that you have resorted to yourself. Please look at these behaviors within the context of your motives. Let's take an obvious example to illustrate our point.

We've said that physical abuse is any form of unwanted physical touch. However, without some consideration of motives, this definition suggests that stepping on someone's toe accidentally is a form of abuse. It is, after all, unwanted physical contact. Yet if you step on someone's toe accidentally, your motive is not to control or to intimidate him or her. The physical contact is accidental; his or her toe just happened to be where you set your foot down.

Similarly, in an attempt to get away from your partner who is yelling at you and blocking your exit from a room, you may push him. This is unwanted physical contact from his point of view, but it is not your intention to control him or to have power over him. You are simply trying to remove yourself from a situation that is not safe for you, either physically or emotionally. Your motive is self-protection, not gaining power and control over your partner.

Often women will describe their motive as simply wanting to be heard and respected—they want to be treated as an equal by their partner. Sometimes women do yell at, swear at, or hit their partners. When women explore the motives behind their behavior, they discover that their ideas, opinions, or feelings have not been acknowledged. Their actions are a response to being repeatedly silenced, a form of abuse that has a significant impact for women. One woman expressed her intentions this way:

*After several hours of grueling verbal attacks from my partner, I lost
it. I walked in the house and he followed. I turned and began to hit
him and scream. Then I realized that this was not me. I stopped,
and started to cry. I did not do any of that to control him. I had not
stooped to his level. I just wanted to be heard and still he was not
hearing me. I realized then he would never hear my voice. For him,
I had no voice.*

—MARIE

At the center of the Power and Control Wheel is the phrase *Power
& Control*. All the abusive behaviors listed are intended to have the
same effect—to control and intimidate. While Marie may have
wanted some control in this particular situation, she was only interested in being heard. She did not want to control her partner. While
her behavior was not desirable, it was not abusive. Her motive was
self-preservation.

If you have resorted to any of this behavior, please don't beat
yourself up. Acknowledge that this is not the way you want to be:
that your motives for this behavior do not come from a controlling
or abusive place. If you have stood up to your partner, you have
probably been aware of how dangerous this can be. We would echo
this caution to you. You may know that fighting back or taking a
stand is potentially dangerous because your partner may have more
physical, financial, or social power than you do. Perhaps your partner has relentlessly attacked and ridiculed you, to the point that you
finally yell back, slam something down, or even push him. He might
then take your actions as an excuse to escalate his abuse to a dangerous level.

HOW CAN I MAKE A
POWER AND CONTROL WHEEL FOR MYSELF?

On the following pages is a Power and Control Wheel for you to complete. Your first step is to name the types of abuse for yourself. Keep in mind that there is no "right" way to do this. For example, some women might combine emotional, intellectual, and verbal abuse together, while other women want to separate these out. Simply decide what works best for you.

There is also no "right" way to fill in the types of abuse with examples of different behaviors or tactics of abuse. If your partner has blocked your exit from the bathroom, you might describe this as physical abuse—it is physically threatening. You might also describe it as emotional abuse—he is holding you hostage. It is also sexual abuse—he is invading you in a physically private space. Simply list the tactic of abuse in whatever category works best for you. You may want to list a tactic or example in more than one category.

HOW MIGHT I FEEL AFTER COMPLETING
MY POWER AND CONTROL WHEEL?

The Power and Control Wheel may have helped you to identify some of your experiences of abuse that you had not recognized before. For example, you might have recognized that your partner was physically and verbally abusive, but had more difficulty naming some of his behavior as financially, intellectually, or sexually abusive.

You may also feel quite overwhelmed at seeing how many kinds of abuse you checked off and how full your Wheel is. Women often say that they didn't realize how pervasive the abuse was until they had completed this exercise.

POWER AND CONTROL WHEEL

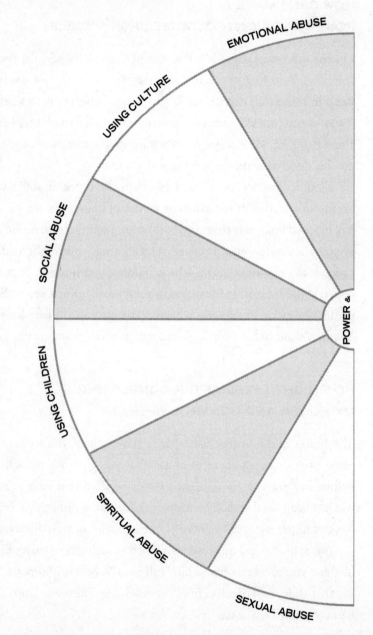

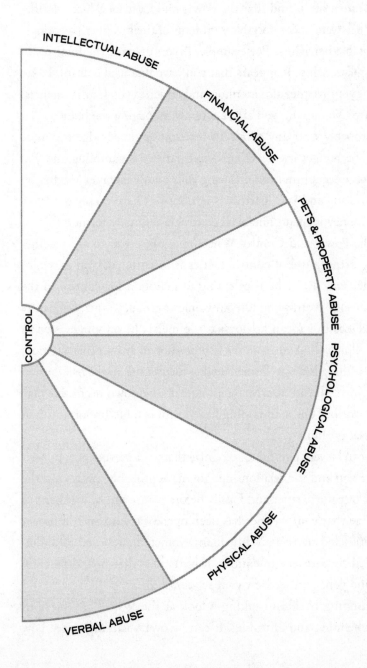

Women often find that the Power and Control Wheel clarifies why they were uncomfortable with some of their partner's seemingly acceptable behaviors. For example, if you manage the finances in your relationship, it appears that you have financial control. However, if your partner also monitors and criticizes you for the financial situation you are in, you aren't actually managing the budget. You are probably worrying about his reaction to your budgeting more than the budget itself. Perhaps your partner is gambling and you cannot prevent him from misusing your family income. Maybe you are working and your partner is not but you have no say over how your money is spent. Financial control takes many forms.

The Power and Control Wheel may cause you to ask whether your partner's use of control tactics is intentional. You may also wonder how aware he is of trying to maintain his control in the relationship. At this point in our women's group, women frequently ask, "Does this mean he doesn't love me? Is he only interested in controlling me?" You are in the best position to answer this question, but one thing is clear: Women tend to focus more on the relationship while men who are abusive focus more on their own needs. He may still love you, but maintaining his control is more important than the relationship.

It can be very painful to recognize that your partner puts himself before you and the relationship. You have probably always put the needs of your partner and family before your own, so it is hard to imagine that your partner has been operating with such different priorities and motives. While many women are relieved to understand their partners' intentions, it hurts to realize how differently you and your partner view your relationship.

Standing back and taking a look at the Wheel can be both overwhelming and affirming. It can be overwhelming to see how pervasive the abuse is in your relationship. But it can also be affirming that what you thought was unacceptable behavior was not only unacceptable but also abusive. It can be devastating to realize that most of your partner's behaviors are abusive and meant to control you while you thought you were working on building a relationship.

While dealing with these difficult realizations, women often express relief because they can finally make sense of their partner's actions. Seeing that your partner is trying to have power and control over you can relieve you of trying to make sense of his erratic and hurtful behavior. He is intent on controlling you, and that is the only way to make sense of his behavior.

We have introduced many new ideas in this chapter, and you may find it a lot to process. Some women have told us that this is a difficult chapter to work through because it makes the abuse seem more concrete and real. While completing the Wheel can be helpful, it can also be alarming and scary. We think you are very courageous to have completed this chapter. We also want you to know that just because you are beginning to see the extent of your partner's abuse does not mean that this is the right time to take any significant action.

Society has a simplistic understanding of abuse that suggests that if you are being abused, you should leave. We know that there are many factors that you are considering and that this decision is complicated. We encourage you to continue to read the book at your own pace and find support and understanding for your situation. Whatever you are experiencing, be gentle with yourself; many women share what you are going through and we understand that there are no simple decisions.

Let's summarize what we have learned in this chapter about the Power and Control Wheel.

The Wheel helps you to identify types and tactics of abuse that you might not have recognized as abuse.

The Wheel illustrates to you that the desire to maintain power and control in the relationship is central to your partner's motives.

The Wheel helps you realize that you may have minimized or disregarded many of these behaviors because, taken alone, they didn't seem that serious. The Wheel allows you to see that it is the sum of all these behaviors that has had an impact on you, and not the severity of any one incident of abuse.

Finally, the list that you compiled shows the tactics that your partner uses to intimidate and control you. Hopefully, this list will help you understand the intent behind your partner's behavior.

In the next chapter we will look at the extent to which, and in what ways, the abuse is affecting you.

FIVE

What's the Abuse Doing to Me?

> Within six months of leaving my husband, Jeff, I was able to stop taking my blood pressure medication. I always thought that this was a permanent condition. I also believed that I had high blood pressure because I couldn't cope with stress. I never thought that it was because of the constant fear and tension of living with an unpredictable and abusive man.
>
> —CLAIRE

Although Claire was never physically assaulted by her partner, the emotional abuse was constant. Every day he found some reason to be critical and argumentative. The stress of living with Jeff took a huge toll on Claire's health.

HOW SERIOUS IS THE ABUSE?

The seriousness of the abuse cannot be judged by the type of abuse you are experiencing, but rather by the impact it is having on you. Often the impact of the abuse is a result of the ongoing, unpredictable, seemingly random actions and reactions of your partner. This reality is invisible to most people. You have probably done a good job of concealing the difficulties you face in your relationship, especially if you have been told the problem is yours. Many women in our groups begin by minimizing or downplaying the abuse. They will say, "It's not that bad. He's never actually hit me. It's mostly been verbal abuse." This type of statement underestimates the harm that all forms of abuse can have on you.

Our society tends to recognize physical abuse because it is perceived to be the most threatening to women. Physical violence is serious and can lead to very painful and even permanent injuries. However, we also want to take seriously the impact of other types of abuse. Let's look at four examples that illustrate the impact of other forms of abuse.

SANDRA

Jim and Sandra have a disagreement while in the car. Jim drives recklessly, causing Sandra to feel fearful and back down from the argument. Jim does not intend to physically harm Sandra, but he does want to frighten her. His recklessness results in an accident. Sandra sustains injuries, including a broken wrist. Do you think the impact on Sandra is any different than if Jim had broken her wrist during an assault?

BRENDA

Dave and Brenda have a disagreement while in the living room. Dave becomes more and more enraged and will not let Brenda leave the room. He finally throws a book at Brenda, which misses her head by only inches. Do you think the impact of this incident is different for Brenda than if Dave had actually hit her head?

REENA

Rajiv and Reena have been together since they were teenagers. Rajiv has never hit Reena, but he is unrelenting in his emotional attacks. He is critical of her appearance and of everything she does. Rajiv's abuse has caused Reena to develop anorexia nervosa. Reena may be starving herself to death. How would you assess the lethality of Rajiv's abuse?

CHARLENE

Ray has closed all the bank accounts and Charlene does not know what he has done with their money. He gives her a limited "allowance" to take care of all the household needs. She is unable to meet all the financial demands that are placed on her as she tries to provide for their three children. Charlene has a serious heart condition that has always been monitored by her doctor, and with the additional financial stresses placed on Charlene because of Ray's abuse, her heart condition has worsened. Her doctor urges her to remove all sources of stress from her life, but Ray refuses all the suggestions she offers to improve the situation. How lethal do you think this situation is?

These scenarios point to an important truth. Abusive men do not need to be physically violent to be abusive. None of the men in these scenarios hit their partner, but the impact of the abuse is quite profound.

No matter how much we counter the societal idea that only physical abuse is serious, many women still feel that the emotional, verbal, financial, and spiritual abuse isn't "that bad" and feel that they should be able to handle it. Taking the impact of all forms of abuse seriously will help to validate all you have been experiencing in your relationship.

WHAT IS THE IMPACT OF THE ABUSE?

In order to keep yourself (and your children) emotionally and physically safe, you've had to pay a great deal of attention to your partner. You probably carefully monitor your partner's moods and behavior. Because you've had to focus on him, you may not have had the opportunity to think about how his abuse affects you.

In our support groups, we invite women to list the ways that their partners' abuse has affected them. We ask them what impact the abuse has had on them. The women brainstorm and fill several pages of flip chart paper with examples of how they have been affected by the abuse.

Below is a list generated by a group of women of the impact the abuse had on them. The list covers every aspect of a woman's life— emotional, intellectual, physical, financial, social, and spiritual. We invite you to read down the list and check off the ways in which you have been affected by your partner's abuse, and we encourage you to add to the list at the bottom.

IMPACT LIST

Because of the abuse, I . . .

○ Wonder if I'm going crazy.
○ Feel isolated.
○ Feel depressed.
○ Feel a lack of interest.
○ Have no energy.
○ Feel disillusioned.
○ Feel distracted.
○ Feel my work is affected.

○ Feel overwhelmed.
○ Want to avoid people/crowds.
○ Lie to people: "I'm fine."
○ Am forced to keep secrets.
○ Feel a lack of support.
○ Feel lonely.
○ Feel suicidal.
○ Am forgetful.

- ○ Feel confused.
- ○ Blank out/black out.
- ○ Feel numb.
- ○ Feel nervous.
- ○ Fear being trapped.
- ○ Experience an emotional roller coaster.
- ○ Feel afraid I won't get out safely.
- ○ Feel vulnerable.
- ○ Feel terrified.
- ○ Have to justify myself/my time.
- ○ Feel paranoid.
- ○ Have panic attacks.
- ○ Feel brainwashed.
- ○ Feel anxious.
- ○ Feel I have to look busy all the time.
- ○ Feel on the alert all the time.
- ○ Smoke more.
- ○ Drink more alcohol.
- ○ Drink more coffee.
- ○ Use street drugs to numb out.
- ○ Rely on prescription drugs to cope.
- ○ Watch TV/Internet more.
- ○ Gamble more.
- ○ Experience insomnia.
- ○ Sleep too much.
- ○ Wake suddenly in the night.
- ○ Wake up in sweats.
- ○ Have bad dreams.
- ○ Can't eat.
- ○ Eat too much.
- ○ Develop ulcers.
- ○ Develop digestive problems.
- ○ Have recurring bladder infections.
- ○ Have muscle pain.
- ○ Have nausea and vomiting.
- ○ Have diarrhea.
- ○ Develop anorexia/bulimia.
- ○ Feel exhausted all the time.
- ○ Get ill often.
- ○ Have heart palpitations.
- ○ Have high blood pressure.
- ○ Have difficulty breathing.
- ○ Have frequent headaches.
- ○ Have recurring yeast infections.
- ○ Was forced to get pregnant.
- ○ Had a forced abortion or miscarriage.
- ○ Am prevented from using birth control.
- ○ Contracted sexually transmitted infections (HIV, Hep C, etc.).
- ○ Experience dizziness.
- ○ Don't like myself.
- ○ Feel ugly.
- ○ Judge myself.
- ○ Feel parts of my personality are flawed.
- ○ Don't value myself.
- ○ Lose myself.
- ○ Lose interest in physical/ sexual intimacy.
- ○ Stop doing what I enjoy.

○ Don't think I deserve to have needs.
○ Do everything for him (for safety).
○ Forget my needs.
○ Am afraid to have my own life, friends.
○ Have little self-respect.
○ Feel guilt about him leaving/ me leaving.
○ Don't feel important.
○ Feel like a failure.
○ Feel incapable.
○ Monitor or censor myself.
○ Feel self-conscious.
○ Question myself.
○ Lose my instincts.
○ Feel embarrassed/ashamed.

○ Doubt myself.
○ Have a hard time trusting men.
○ Feel callous.
○ Feel angry.
○ Yell at children/pets.
○ Feel angry at myself.
○ Want to hurt him.
○ Feel like a prostitute.
○ Become bankrupt.
○ Lose my home.
○ Fall into poverty.
○ Lose my faith community.
○ Lose my faith.
○ Have my creativity stifled.
○ _____
○ _____
○ _____

Most women are shocked to see the many ways in which the abuse has affected them. This list can be very affirming. Maybe you've been worried that there is something seriously wrong with you because you have felt forgetful, confused, depressed, or constantly sick. This list helps to explain your concerns as the impacts of abuse. It may also help you to understand why you're so exhausted—look at all that you've been coping with! We hope you are beginning to recognize that these are normal human responses to all the abuse you have been experiencing.

So many women have expressed concern to us about how the abuse has affected their mental health, which we want to explore in more detail. Women describe experiencing high levels of anxiety or depression. Some women suffer with panic attacks and may become fearful of leaving their home. Some women feel confused, forgetful, or overwhelmed. Some women have thoughts of suicide. Have you ever wondered if you are "going crazy"? We don't think you are "crazy," but your partner's behavior is certainly crazy making! If you have worried about whether there is something wrong with you, maybe a question you could ask yourself is, "Do I think my mental health would be a concern if I were with a loving and supportive partner?" If you answer "no" to this question, then maybe instead of thinking that there is something wrong with you, you are able to see that your "symptoms" are normal responses to experiencing abuse. Sometimes professionals mistake the impact of abuse for mental illness and women can get labels attached to them that may not be helpful. If your mental health professional really understood the stress and "crazy-making" behavior you live with, how would this affect how you are seen and understood?

Below, some women share how the fear of living with an abusive partner has affected their mental well-being.

After I moved to the women's shelter, I knew I was depressed and almost had a mental breakdown. But now I realize it was caused by the fear I had of my partner. That fear was there even after I separated from him. I would wake up in the night with that fear, thinking I was back at home. It took me a year to stop feeling that.

—JEWEL

A lot of stuff still triggers me. When I was with my partner, I wasn't allowed to watch the television loudly; even now if my son puts the volume up, I panic and tell him to put the volume down. That fear is still there. It affects you mentally, even though you are out of that cycle—it is still there.

—ESTHER

We went over to his parents' house for dinner. As soon as I took off my coat, I realized I was dressed wrong. I was wearing jeans but his mom was dressed up. He glared at me. Through dinner, I could hardly follow the conversation and it was really hard to eat. All I could think about was as soon as we got in the car, he was going to blow.

—CORA

We also want to take a moment to highlight another impact of abuse that women share with us—using drugs or alcohol to try to cope with abuse. If you have used alcohol, prescription medication, or street drugs to try to numb the physical and emotional pain or stay safe, you are not alone. Although there are negative stereotypes of women with "addiction issues," the women we have met do not fit these stereotypes. They are women from all walks of life, trying to survive their partners' abuse.

There were several points in the relationship where everything seemed completely hopeless. I would find myself sitting with a bottle of rum, it was that bad. I know now that I drank to try to stop the emotional and physical pain.

—ISABELLA

Some women describe using substances as a safety strategy to reduce the risks of abuse.

The relationship wasn't good and it became a safety strategy to drink with him because if I drank with him he didn't yell and scream at me and freak out as much.

—SAMI

Women have also told us that they know it's not safe to say no to what their partners are doing to them. Using substances can help them numb those experiences.

> *For me, I used to get high behind his back. He didn't know it, but I could take all his demands, and I was like, "Yeah sure, let's have sex." I had to put up with him.*
>
> —DAWN

Perhaps your partner or others have used your substance use against you rather than seeing it as a coping strategy. Maybe it's been suggested to you that the real problem in the relationship is your substance use. Maybe you've started to think that's true.

> *I am hopelessly addicted to marijuana and that's how I blocked it out. I think the drugs really helped in keeping me with him, then I thought it was my fault.*
>
> —APRIL

Once women find safety or support, they often find their use of drugs or alcohol diminishes or disappears. In our experience, not all service providers understand the links between women's use of substances and abuse. Finding support from someone who does understand these links can make a big difference in a woman's life.

AM I BEING BRAINWASHED?

Many abusive men use brainwashing strategies to control their partners and ensure that women comply with their demands. Does this seem like extreme language to use to describe your partner's intentions? It may be difficult to learn that your partner has been controlling you in this way, but hopefully this helps you to put a name to some of your experiences.

We use the term *brainwashing* to describe what happens when an abusive man systematically controls his partner by employing a set of strategies aimed at breaking down her physical and mental defenses. Elements of brainwashing include the prolonged use of sleep deprivation, belittling and humiliation, enforcing trivial demands, name-calling, and enforcing his values and beliefs. Brainwashing is intended to weaken and diminish the woman, leaving her isolated and dependent.

Researchers have drawn parallels between the tactics used in prisoner-of-war camps to brainwash and break down their prisoners and the strategies that abusive men use to control their partners. The similarities between the tactics used by interrogators and those used by abusive men point to the profound effect that mental and emotional abuse can have on an individual. You may wonder why we draw these parallels. You certainly aren't a prisoner of war. You may get up and go to work each day, conducting yourself competently and independently. You may have many friends with whom you stay in touch. You may be responsible for all the financial management in your family. We know how strong and capable women who live with abuse really are; not for a moment would we suggest that you are weak or incapable. In the same way, your partner's motives are probably not identical to those of an interrogator.

Although not identical, we invite you to see any similarities between brainwashing and the strategies that your partner has used. Some of the strategies are subtle, such as constantly criticizing your driving until you no longer want to drive, but they have significant impacts. You may find that it undermines your confidence, challenges your competence, wears you down so you no longer resist, and leaves you completely exhausted.

Below we provide you with some examples of how men have used brainwashing strategies. A common brainwashing strategy used by abusive men is sleep deprivation, which is intended to weaken your mental and physical ability to resist and maintain his control over you.

COLLEEN

Colleen is exhausted. For the third night in a row, her partner has kept her up until 2:00 a.m., berating her for making plans to spend a weekend with her family. This is a common occurrence for Colleen. Sometimes, just as she's falling off to sleep, he'll insist on discussing something with her. Colleen can't remember the last time she had enough sleep. She finds herself giving in more to her partner's demands as she is too exhausted to disagree.

Another common brainwashing strategy is degradation and humiliation. Women are belittled and shamed until they no longer stand up for themselves; to do so is too dangerous. Humiliation is a powerful tool in controlling someone. Here is an example of how one woman's partner used this tactic.

BETHANY

Russell is an opinionated person who is quite vocal about his ideas in social settings. Bethany is often embarrassed by the extreme statements that Russell makes at parties. On a number of occasions in the past, Bethany has attempted to moderate Russell's extreme views with her own more moderate statements. Each time Bethany does this, however, Russell embarrasses her by commenting that she didn't finish college. Now Bethany questions her own intelligence and remains silent at parties.

A third element of brainwashing is enforcing trivial demands and insisting on compliance. A woman finds herself trying to anticipate his every need, yet never succeeding. Eventually women are afraid to think and act for themselves and do whatever they are told to avoid an explosion. Here is an example of how this tactic can be used by an abusive man.

JULIA

Brent insists on the house being spotless and everything being in its designated place. Over time, Brent changes the rules about where things are to go. Lately Julia feels panicked when she comes home from work. She second-guesses everything she does. One night, after dinner, she is trying to load the dishwasher the way Brent insists on it being done. She feels like she's having a panic attack: She is paralyzed with fear knowing that, no matter what she does, he could explode.

These examples illustrate the serious nature of your experiences of mental and emotional abuse and identify common reactions to this abuse. They describe the impact that tactics such as induced exhaustion, threats of degradation, or the enforcement of trivial demands may be having on your mental or physical well-being.

We have included this information to show you how, in a situation of danger, people are forced to behave in ways that conflict with their true self. Your self is not lost, but you bury it in order to protect yourself from the emotional, sexual, physical, mental, and verbal attacks. You may also have to go along with your partner's needs and demands, even if your heart isn't in it. Some women have felt forced to break the law or compromise their values. Prisoners of war respond the same way: They modify their behavior to keep themselves safe. As with prisoners of war, you have found strategies to keep your children and yourself as safe as possible in an unpredictable situation. Such strategies show wisdom and courage on your part.

WILL I ALWAYS FEEL THIS BAD?

Once again, it may be overwhelming or liberating or both to look at the work you have done in this chapter. You may be overwhelmed at your discovery of how much your partner's abuse has affected you. You may feel very sad or angry. You may, however, feel liberated at discovering an explanation for some of the things you have been experiencing. It may be helpful to realize that the reasons you eat, sleep, or drink too much can be found in the abuse you have been living with.

Your partner's abuse has had a serious impact on you, leaving you feeling tired, confused, and perhaps even ill. Women wonder if they will always feel as bad as they do now. Most women find that, once they have a break from the abuse, many of the negative effects go away. Although it can sometimes take a few months, women have described being able to sleep properly once again or having their blood pressure go back down to normal.

We realize that it may not be possible right now to escape your partner's abuse either temporarily or permanently. However, there are some things you can do to try to take care of yourself and lessen the impact of the abuse. Some women do this by attending a women's support group in order to share their experiences. Other women take advantage of opportunities to have time for themselves, even if it means just taking the dog for a walk. One woman we know volunteers outside her home because she feels valued by the staff and other volunteers. Receiving affirmation from outside sources has helped to keep her partner's unrelenting criticism in perspective.

Take some time to appreciate your ability to survive such a difficult relationship, especially one that impacts you in so many ways. Realizing what a difficult situation you are in and taking care of yourself will not change the situation. However, focusing on yourself when you can may at least give you the energy to take on the larger challenges that face you.

If it seems impossible to find any time, or you feel too exhausted to do anything, please be patient with yourself. Not judging yourself is a very important way of taking care of yourself.

We will explore these ideas further in the next chapter as we look more deeply at what is happening to you in your relationship.

SIX

Am I Responsible for the Abuse?

I didn't like the way I behaved in my marriage. I always felt like I was "nagging" and making matters worse. I really tried hard to drop things or leave issues alone. I kept trying to change the way I was, believing that I was partly responsible for the mess we were in.

—JANET

AM I TO BLAME?

Women often wonder if they are responsible for the problems in their relationship. They wonder if they are not coping well or if they are somehow making the situation worse. In this chapter, we hope to offer more positive ways of understanding yourself and how you are responding in your relationship. Let's look at some examples.

PAM

Pam has just finished reading another self-help book about relationships. She has been reflecting on the number of men that she has been with who have been hurtful to her, including her current partner. She is wondering if she's attracted to abusive men. With the help of the book she's reading, she has concluded that the abuse she experienced as a child has left her believing that abuse is normal in relationships. She decides that she must focus on healing herself from her past experiences.

Many self-help books are written primarily for women seeking answers to their own unhappiness, relationship problems, or specific issues such as anger or intimacy. Many of these books come from the position that women are responsible for the problem. Some books even suggest that women are attracted to abuse or think abuse is "normal." These books suggest that once a woman "fixes" herself, her relationship will be enhanced and the problems will disappear.

Based on the advice of self-help books, Pam concludes that she is attracted to abusive men, but this ignores the tactics her partner used in the honeymoon phase of the Cycle. Her partner probably initially behaved in a respectful, considerate, and loving manner, at which point Pam committed herself to the relationship. Pam saw qualities in her partner that were positive. She was attracted to these positive qualities in her partner; she was not attracted to the abuse.

In addition, if Pam thought abuse was normal, she would not be trying to bring about change in her relationship. She does know what qualities in a partner she wants and deserves, and she does not believe abuse is normal. Furthermore, if Pam does focus on her childhood experiences, she may be less guarded about her current safety. Such a focus allows her partner to exploit the idea that the problem lies in her "dysfunctional" childhood rather than in his need to control her. She is made to feel responsible for the difficulties in the relationship.

As I began to look at sexual abuse from my past, my partner's abuse grew worse. I felt I was opening up a Pandora's box. He began to blame all the problems of our marriage on my dysfunctional childhood. The focus and blame switched to me. It kept him in control and me confused. After the divorce is final, I hope to be able to go back and heal from the sexual abuse and put those experiences behind me.

—CARLA

This book does not focus on your childhood experiences but rather on your current experiences of abuse from your partner. This is not because we wish to minimize the abuse you may have suffered in childhood or because we deem it unimportant, but because we believe it is more helpful to focus first and foremost on your current situation. It can be dangerous to focus too much on your childhood if you are with a partner who is abusive. You may reveal very painful stories to him only to have him use these against you. Being told that you deserved to be treated the way your mother treated you or having him reenact something abusive your father did can be devastating. In the final analysis, whether or not you were abused as a child does not alter your current reality of abuse. You do not want your past to serve as an excuse for your partner's current behavior. The focus needs to be on your partner and his responsibility for his behavior. It can be dangerous if he places the responsibility on you.

NANCY

Nancy has been with her abusive partner for four years. She recently confided in a friend that she was very unhappy in her relationship, that her husband never listens to her. Her friend suggested that Nancy is too focused on how she would like her partner to be and does not accept him as he is. Because of this, she is never satisfied. Nancy vows to be less critical of her partner. She also tells her mother about her resolve to be more accepting. Her mother enthusiastically approves of her decision, stating that her partner works hard for his family and needs her unconditional support.

Nancy's friend fails to pay attention to the context in which Nancy lives, which is a context of abuse. Once we understand Nancy's experience in terms of the impact of abuse—her lack of freedom to express herself and her needs without being criticized and ridiculed—Nancy's need to focus on her partner's behavior makes sense. While her friend has interpreted Nancy's behavior as problematic, we understand Nancy's situation differently.

Nancy has clear and reasonable expectations of her partner—that he be respectful and contribute to the relationship. Indeed, she is focused on how she would like her partner to be because, as long as he is abusive, she is being hurt and oppressed. It makes sense to focus on his changing, because his current behavior is unacceptable.

However, Nancy's partner perpetuates the idea that, if she were satisfied with the way things are, he wouldn't "lose his temper." Nancy then resolves to be less critical, hoping that this will solve the abuse and that he will not explode again. Nancy ends up taking responsibility for his behavior.

Her mother's affirmation of Nancy's resolution to be more accepting of her partner conforms to many societal assumptions about a woman's role in a relationship. Women are supposed to nurture their partner's ego and be unconditionally supportive. Furthermore, women are supposed to be grateful for a man's attention, however limited that is, and the financial support he provides. If women "complain," they are unfeminine, selfish, demanding, and hard to please. The assumption is that men are abusive because their partners are difficult or demanding. This assumption leaves women feeling responsible for the abuse.

Family and friends may blame women for the abuse in their relationship. They reinforce the idea that, if relationships are to improve, women must accommodate and compromise. This incorrect assumption presumes that women can effect change with a man whose primary interest is staying in control of the relationship. Nothing a woman does will make a lasting difference unless her partner is willing to let go of his desire for power and control.

SANDRA

Sandra is feeling unappreciated in her relationship. She finds her partner is often disrespectful of her. She finally persuades him to go with her for marriage counseling. The therapist focuses on Sandra's behavior and suggests that she does not have very good boundaries for herself. Sandra is told that she needs to get a lot clearer with her partner about what is disturbing for her in the relationship. He suggests she needs to be a lot more assertive and say "no" to her partner's criticisms and unreasonable demands. The therapist believes that Sandra's low self-esteem is the source of the problem. Sandra and her partner leave the counselor's office and return two weeks later. Sandra now describes an instance in which she tried to be more assertive. Her partner didn't speak to her for two days. The therapist states that perhaps Sandra was too aggressive in making her needs known. Furthermore, change is difficult, asserts the therapist, and so her partner was just reacting normally to a change in their communication patterns.

Many of the observations we made about Nancy's situation also apply to Sandra. Let's focus specifically on the advice Sandra received about setting boundaries. We think that Sandra has been very wise because she knows that saying "no" or trying to set boundaries with a controlling partner is unsafe. With a partner who is respectful, of course, women can expect to set boundaries without consequence (although there is usually less need to do so in a respectful relationship). However, when a partner intends to remain in charge, he perceives her saying "no" as a threat to his control. He is likely to attack the "boundary" in order to regain control.

Sandra needed her counselor to affirm that it wasn't safe to set boundaries and that boundaries are not the issue. She had shown great wisdom and insight in the past by not asserting herself and her needs. While she has every right to express herself, as long as her partner is abusive, she will have to conceal herself and her needs. Sandra has experienced the consequences of disagreeing with him, expressing her opinion, or saying "no" to something he is doing. She may never have felt physically threatened by her partner, but the emotional attacks on her self-identity make her fear his unpredictable responses. This lack of safety to express herself forces Sandra to use strategies to keep herself protected, sometimes even prompting Sandra to say and do things that are against her own values and principles. For example, because Sandra's partner insists on lying to the government about his income, she is forced to misrepresent herself on her tax return even though this really upsets her and makes her feel dishonest. Some would interpret this as "unassertive" or "cowardly" behavior on Sandra's part because she does not stand up for what she believes in, but we know Sandra has made a wise choice within the context of abuse. We understand Sandra's compliant behavior not as the cause of the abuse but rather as part of the impact of living with an abusive man.

As you can see by these examples, when the impact of abuse is not taken into account, the problem is often interpreted as a weakness or deficit in the woman—such as Pam's childhood abuse or

Nancy's criticism of her partner. Often what women like Sandra have consciously or unconsciously used as a safety strategy, such as not setting limits or saying "no" to her partner, is misinterpreted as her problem.

One final assumption we challenge is the notion that Sandra's low self-esteem causes the abuse. Many women have been convinced by professionals and others that low self-esteem is the problem, but it is not. We believe that the reverse is true—the way you feel about yourself is related to how your partner has treated you. Some women have been told that if they "work on their self-esteem," their relationship will improve. If your partner is abusive, this is not true. It is hard to hold on to a positive image of yourself while you are with your partner. He does not want you to feel good about yourself.

You might ask yourself, "Did I feel better about myself before I was involved with this partner or at the beginning of this relationship?" If you answer "yes" to this question, we hope you see that it is your partner's abuse that has negatively affected how you feel about yourself. If you say "no" to this question, perhaps it is because you entered the relationship with a harmed sense of self to begin with. It is not unusual for a person to come out of a bad childhood or bad relationship not feeling good about themselves. A loving, respectful partner helps us to see the best in ourselves and is protective and kind about our vulnerabilities. If your partner is abusive, he has probably used those vulnerabilities against you and made you feel like you deserved the abuse. Your vulnerability is no reason or explanation for your partner's abuse.

For these reasons, we do not think of women as having "poor self-esteem." You may not feel that you have much self-worth, but this is the result of your partner manipulating your ideas about yourself—not some sort of inherent weakness or problem that you have.

IS THERE ANOTHER WAY TO LOOK AT
MY BEHAVIOR?

We would like to introduce another exercise intended to help you to "reframe" some of the ways in which you (or others) have interpreted your motives and behavior. By *reframing*, we mean offering you a different way to think about your behavior. For example, if you have been told you are "not assertive enough," reframing helps you to understand this differently and say, "I need to be cautious in my relationship."

The Reframing Exercise describes "your problem" in a new light. It offers three alternative explanations for women's reaction to abuse: safety strategy, strength, and impact.

This exercise will help you to see that some of what you do is intended to try to keep yourself safe. We call these safety strategies. You may also realize that what you do shows great strength of character on your part rather than demonstrating some sort of problem or shortcoming. Finally, some of what you do may simply be a result of the abuse or the impact of the abuse.

In the chart on the next page, we first list negative ideas that women sometimes have about themselves or that are suggested to them by others. We then offer alternative ways of understanding these feelings and behaviors. We have left blank spaces at the end of the chart for you to write additional descriptions of your motives and behaviors, either held by you or placed on you by others. These descriptions imply that you are responsible for the problem. Reframing them to reflect a more accurate interpretation of your intentions will help you to see that your behavior is not the problem that your partner would have you believe. Instead, you will see that you have been acting wisely in a situation of abuse.

DIAGRAM 6.1: REFRAMING EXERCISE

NEGATIVE DESCRIPTION	SAFETY STRATEGY	STRENGTH	IMPACT
"You're a troublemaker"	I need to defend myself against my partner's accusations	I have my own opinions and ideas	I'm made to feel responsible for problems
"You can't handle conflict"	I watch out for my emotional and physical well-being	I'm able to negotiate and compromise in my relationships	My experiences of abuse have made me afraid of conflict
"You're too dependent on your partner"	I know my independence threatens my partner's need to control me	I'm interested in my partner and our relationship	My partner has forced me to be dependent (socially, financially, etc.)
"Your expectations are too low"	I know it is unsafe to state my expectations	I am a tolerant person	My partner does not meet my expectations so I am forced to lower them
"You are not assertive enough"	I know it is unsafe to express my needs or opinions	I am respectful of others	My experiences of abuse have made me cautious
"You nag too much"	I know I have to remind my partner or I will be blamed for his forgetfulness	I'm asking my partner to be responsible for his part in the relationship	I have to repeat myself in order to be heard
"You love too much"	I have to be loving so he won't become angry and abusive	I am a caring, compassionate person	The honeymoon phase of the Cycle keeps me engaged in the relationship
"You pay too much attention to your partner's feelings"	I focus on my partner's moods to anticipate explosions	I care about my partner	I am unable to pay attention to my personal needs

continues on next page . . .

NEGATIVE DESCRIPTION	SAFETY STRATEGY	STRENGTH	IMPACT

Hopefully, the Reframing Exercise has helped you to appreciate your strengths, despite the fact that some people may see them as faults. Sometimes other people, even if they care for you, do not understand the context of abuse and the importance of using strategies and wisdom to protect yourself and your children.

The following example further illustrates how some "solutions" can be dangerous. Here is what one woman was instructed to do by her therapist (who knew she lived with an abusive partner):

> **THERAPIST:** When he gets angry, you've got to just step up to the line and assert yourself. Don't let him push you off that line.

THE THERAPIST HOLDS THE FOLLOWING ASSUMPTIONS:

- The woman is responsible for the problem.
- She's not assertive enough.
- She lets herself be pushed around.

- Her partner gets upset and she backs away. He's learned he can get away with this behavior. It is her responsibility to teach him he can't.
- She's letting her partner take advantage of her and take control. If she takes control, he'll respect her more (i.e., he won't be angry).

Perhaps you have heard the messages of responsibility so often that they feel like your own ideas. This woman felt compelled to accept the following ideas, even though they put her at risk:

- I need to try harder.
- I should understand what he's going through.
- He's in pain, too—I need to be more patient.
- I've got to make this work.
- If only I were stronger.
- If only I had higher self-esteem.
- If only I were more assertive.
- I need to focus on the future rather than holding on to the past.

In contrast to the therapist, here's how we might interpret this woman's intentions and behaviors if we assume she is wise and trying to stay safe:

- She has already tried in hundreds of ways to prevent or decrease his anger, and the response is always abusive.
- She is smart to move away from "the line" in a confrontation because she has been injured physically and emotionally when she has tried to defend herself.

 • She has the right to assert herself, but for her safety, she chooses
   to go along with her partner's demands.

The therapist in this case was irresponsible. He did not believe
that the woman was at risk, and because she was willing to try any
suggested action to stop the abuse, she was easy to work with. We
hope that this story will give you the affirmation and courage you
need to disregard the advice of anyone who doesn't believe your
experience and affirm you in your decisions.

We encourage you to continue using the Reframing Exercise to
understand your experiences. Practice making a mental "flip" whenever someone offers an explanation or description of you that suggests you are the problem. Ask yourself, "Is there a more accurate
way to describe my motives and behavior that includes the impact
of the abuse?"

SO WHO IS RESPONSIBLE?

This chapter may have been difficult for you to work through. If
you have always believed that you were responsible for the problems
in the relationship, it can be challenging to start thinking in a new
way. As a woman, you were raised to pay a lot of attention to others
and to your relationship. You know how to take care of the people
around you. Because of this, you have always been very willing to
work on your relationship and to take responsibility for your actions.
The end result is that you may have accepted more than your share
of the blame.

Until now you may have felt that, since the problem lies with
you, you have some power to change it. But no matter what you
have done to deal with a problem, your partner has sabotaged it,

undermined your efforts, distorted the reality, or shifted the problem back on to you. It is painful to realize that you do not have the power to stop your partner's abuse. Only he has the ability to stop being abusive.

We know that you are not perfect. You have perhaps done things in your relationship that you do not feel good about. However, if your partner is abusive, that is the problem you and others need to remain focused on.

We have spent the first six chapters talking about your partner's behavior and your experiences of abuse. While you may be gaining a clearer picture of the different kinds of abuse your partner employs and the effect this abuse has on you, you no doubt have deeper questions you would like to address. Most women want to know why their partner behaves the way he does. Many women also ask questions about how the abuse is affecting their children. We will turn to these questions in the next two chapters.

SEVEN

Why Is My Partner Abusive?

> My husband insisted that he could do the housework better
> than I could. When he did do the housework, he took all day
> and ignored everything and everyone else. He wouldn't re-
> spond to the kids, and we were just supposed to stay out of
> his way. Then he insisted that we keep the house clean, with
> nothing out of place. With two young children, this was an
> impossible expectation. The clean house was just another
> way to show me he was superior and was also an excuse to
> verbally attack me when it got messy.
>
> —PATRICIA

WHY IS MY PARTNER LIKE THIS?

No doubt you have spent a lot of time and energy trying to figure out
what causes your partner to behave the way he does. Listed below are
some common explanations that women struggle with as they try to
make sense of their partner's behavior. Some may sound familiar to you.

1. My partner has a problem with his anger (or has a bad temper)
   and sometimes he simply loses control.
2. My partner lives with a lot of stress because of his work (or lack
   of work), and his explosions are a result of this stress.
3. My partner suffers from some form of mental illness (depression,
   bipolar, borderline personality disorder). He can't help the way
   he behaves.

4. My partner witnessed his father abusing his mother and is repeating the pattern.
5. My partner was abused as a child.
6. My partner is addicted to drugs or alcohol and would stop being abusive if he were clean and sober.
7. My partner and I have different styles for dealing with conflict.

Although these are common explanations in our culture, they are not excuses for your partner's behavior. Indeed, your partner may be stressed or depressed or come from an abusive or dysfunctional home, but none of these explanations fully describes or justifies your partner's abusive behavior. Let's look more closely at each of them.

1. My Partner Has a Problem with Anger.

It is a common idea that abusive men have a problem with anger and therefore simply lose control sometimes and become abusive. There are two main concerns about this explanation about your partner's abuse. First, as we have learned through the Cycle of Abuse and the Power and Control Wheel, anger is just one of many tactics of abuse. Second, your partner isn't out of control—he is in control. You can test this theory by thinking about a time when your partner was angry at someone else and yet didn't become abusive. For example, has your partner ever been angry with his boss and become explosive? Would he treat his boss with the same level of abuse he directs toward you?

Most women know that their partners would never swear at, yell at, or hit a boss or co-worker. If your partner is able to "control" himself in his workplace, he is able to control himself at home. Although your partner's behavior may seem to be out of control, he is actually using his anger to intimidate you and regain control over you.

2. My Partner Lives with a Lot of Stress.

Your partner may live with a lot of stress. These days, many people do. Stop and think about all the sources of stress in your life (e.g., work, parenting, household responsibilities, extended family, dealing with an abusive man). Even though you also live with stress, you are not being abusive. Living with stress is never an excuse for being abusive.

3. My Partner Is Mentally Ill.

Sometimes women think their partner must be mentally ill because his behavior is so bizarre or erratic. Some abusive men are even diagnosed by doctors or counselors with some form of mental illness. Ask yourself two questions:

First, does your partner display this "abnormal" behavior with everyone or just with you? Is he depressed around or paranoid with other people? If he does not consistently display "abnormal" behavior, he may not be mentally ill.

Second, does having a mental illness give someone permission to be abusive? In our work with women, we find that many of them struggle with depression and yet they are not abusive. Having a mental illness and being abusive are two separate issues.

4. My Partner Witnessed His Father Abusing His Mother.

Some people think we are doomed to repeat the failures of our parents but this is not true. Your partner might explain his abuse because he saw his father abuse his mother. While this is important information, it is not an excuse. He's an adult and he is responsible for his own behavior. He needs to understand how his actions impact you and your children and make changes so you feel safe and cared for.

5. My Partner Was Abused as a Child.

You might have a lot of compassion for your partner if he experienced abuse as a child. It is tragic if your partner was abused as a child. But that is no excuse for his abusing you. What he does now is his choice. He is responsible for his behavior. Do you know of others who were abused as children yet who are not abusive to their partners (e.g., a friend or yourself)? We have supported many women who were abused as children and are now determined to not hurt anyone the way they were hurt.

You might ask yourself if he is working hard to heal from his experiences of abuse or if he is using it to justify his abuse of you. Or you might ask yourself, does your partner bring up his childhood abuse to make you feel sorry for him? Both of these are examples of your safety taking a backseat to his past pain.

6. My Partner Is Addicted to Drugs or Alcohol.

If your partner has an addiction, that can be a serious problem. His abuse, however, is a separate issue. If you're finding other parts of this book helpful, it is likely that your partner is abusive. Your partner may have both issues and that can lead to an even more dangerous situation for you. Women report that the explosion phase can be more severe when their partners are drinking or using drugs, but even when they are not using, they continue to be controlling in less obvious ways throughout the Cycle. Many women have found that even after their partner gets sober, he continues to be abusive, which might help you to see that his addiction and abuse are two separate issues. Some research even shows that abusive men who go to addiction treatment programs become more abusive. This might be because addiction treatment encourages people to focus on themselves, not on the impact that they are having on others. It is wise for you to be cautious about treatment programs if your partner is abusive.

7. My Partner Has a Different Style for Dealing with Conflict Than I Do.

Abuse is never an acceptable "style" of conflict resolution. Conflict means disagreement; both partners have an equal opportunity to express themselves, without fear of the repercussions. When two people try to resolve conflict, neither leaves the discussion feeling attacked, intimidated, or humiliated. It's not conflict if you feel attacked and silenced—it's abuse.

WHAT BELIEF SYSTEM IS HELD BY ABUSIVE MEN?

A study conducted at the University of British Columbia with men who had completed a counseling program for abuse offers an insightful explanation for abusive men's behavior. Through their extensive interviews, researchers found that abusive men consistently communicated similar beliefs and ideas. The beliefs they held supported their actions to use abusive tactics to maintain power and control over their partner.[5]

---

5 M. N. Russell and J. Frohberg, *Comparison of Confronting Abusive Beliefs and Anger Management Treatments for Assaultive Males* (Vancouver: University of British Columbia, 1995).

The research pointed to three key ideas that make up the belief system of abusive men. Women have consistently expressed to us that these three ideas accurately reflect their partner's beliefs and behaviors. The beliefs are:

- He is *central* in the relationship.
- He is *superior* in the relationship.
- He is *deserving* of many privileges within the relationship.

In Chapter 4, we stated that the purpose of your partner's behavior is to maintain power and control over you. Now we want to explore the beliefs your partner holds that lead him to think he has a "right" to hold power and control over you and is entitled to have his needs met, often at your expense. Let's look at each of these beliefs, along with some specific attitudes or behaviors that are a result of these beliefs. Not all of these examples will reflect your experience, but some may be familiar.

CENTRAL

- His work, hobbies, and interests are more important than yours.
- His needs come before yours or your children's.
- He demands your attention whenever he wants it.
- He is active with the children, but only when it makes him look good.
- He only does what he's interested in (social events, child care, etc.).
- He does housework, and then expects a lot of praise.
- The household operates according to his timetable (e.g., dinner is ready when he wants it).
- Everything needs to be scheduled around his needs.

SUPERIOR

- In anything that is "important," he is better than you are.
- He criticizes or puts you down.
- He thinks he is smarter than you are.
- His opinions are more valuable than yours.
- He thinks he is superior to other people.
- His work is more important than your work.
- He devalues or dismisses what you do (at home or work).

DESERVING

- He feels he has a right to rest or relaxation.
- He expects you to do more of the housework.
- He expects praise for every household task he does.
- He expects you to do more of the parenting.
- He expects sex whenever he wants it.
- He expects to be taken care of when he is sick.
- He expects to be fed and cared for.

Abusive men will use any tactic to enforce their desire to be central, superior, and deserving in the relationship. Let's look at some examples of how this belief system allows for his abusive behavior.

Centrality

Darlene and her two-year-old daughter, Christie, are sick with the flu. Because Darlene needs to go to bed, she asks Tom to stay up to care for their daughter. Tom has an early morning meeting and does not want to stay up late. Darlene tries to explain that she is really quite ill and unable to care for Christie.

Tom becomes angry and accuses her of not being supportive of his work. Clearly she has no idea how demanding and stressful his job is. Why should he have to put up with more demands at home? She never thinks about anybody but herself. He suggests that she isn't really that sick and is just being selfish. When Darlene defends herself, Tom's abuse escalates until he calls her a "selfish bitch" and a "lazy mother." He storms out of the house and, when he returns, goes straight to bed. Darlene is left to care for Christie.

Because Tom thinks his needs are central, he puts himself before his partner's or his daughter's needs. Tom uses verbal accusations, threatening behavior, and name-calling to avoid being responsible to his partner or his child and to maintain his centrality in the household.

Superiority

Gail and Doug need a new vehicle. Gail looks online every day for reasonably priced family cars and often points out cars that she thinks they can afford. Doug is never very interested in her suggestions. One day Doug comes home with a new truck. The truck cost significantly more than they had budgeted and it is not the "family car" Gail thought they had agreed to purchase.

When Gail questions Doug's actions, he becomes aggressive. She asks why they didn't go look at some of the cars together. He tells her that she doesn't know anything about cars and everything she was looking at was "crap." When Gail discovers that the new truck means $600 a month in loan repayments, she becomes furious. She feels they are already burdened by too much debt. He tells her that, if she wasn't such a coward, she would ask her boss for a raise and then they wouldn't have any money problems.

Gail reminds Doug that their bad financial situation is a result of the debt he brought into the marriage. He is furious at her for "bringing up the past" and shoves her against the wall. She pushes him back and he grabs her hair and bangs her head into the wall. Frightened and hurt, Gail decides to drop it and leaves the room.

Doug's belief that he has a superior knowledge of vehicles allows him to make a unilateral decision and buy a truck without first consulting Gail. He also makes himself superior by belittling Gail's efforts and knowledge. Furthermore, by accusing Gail of being responsible for their financial difficulties, he shifts the problem to Gail's "inferior" ability to manage her workplace. By accusing her of bringing up the past and physically abusing her, he silences Gail's protest. He can interpret this as "winning," thus ensuring his superior status. Doug uses financial, verbal, and physical abuse to maintain his superiority.

Deserving

Tanya asks Greg if he has had any thoughts about his upcoming vacation time. She is hoping that the whole family can go camping together. Greg complains that such a trip would not be relaxing for him. He wants to take his two weeks and go fishing with some friends. Tanya reacts strongly to this idea. She wants some "family time" and doesn't want to be left alone with three children. He argues that he works hard and needs his vacation to be a vacation. She insists that she also works hard raising the children. He laughs at her and tells her that she doesn't know what hard work is.

Tanya suggests that he go fishing for part of the time and camp with the family for the remainder of his vacation. He tells her that if he can't go fishing for all of it, there's no point in going for any of it. Clearly feeling sorry for himself, Greg is moody for the next week and hardly speaks to Tanya or the children. As his vacation time approaches, Tanya realizes that he's going to make camping miserable for the family and suggests that he go on the fishing trip. He readily agrees and his mood immediately improves.

Greg believes that he deserves a vacation from all of life's responsibilities—something Tanya never gets to have. She is forced to put her needs aside because he considers them unimportant. Tanya and the children are not included in Greg's decision making because, from his perspective, only he deserves a holiday. He belittles Tanya's hard work and the needs of the family as a way of ensuring that he can justify his deservedness. Greg uses emotional abuse to get his way.

WHY DOESN'T HE TREAT ME WITH RESPECT?

The above examples demonstrate that abusive men are not thinking about respect; they are thinking about control. Their belief system—central, superior, and deserving—gives them the "right" to control their partners and justify using whatever tactics are necessary to maintain their position of power. An abusive man will use whatever forms of abuse he needs to get what he wants.

In contrast to the above power and control belief system that allows men to be central, superior, and deserving is the "relationship" belief system held by respectful individuals. People living within a relationship belief system are interested in having:

- *Connection* with their partner.
- *Equality* with their partner.
- *Mutuality* with their partner.

The diagram below compares these two belief systems.

DIAGRAM 7.1: CONTRASTING BELIEF SYSTEMS

POWER AND CONTROL BELIEF SYSTEM	RELATIONSHIP BELIEF SYSTEM
Central	Connected
Superior	Equal
Deserving	Mutual

Here are some attitudes or actions that reflect a relationship belief system:

CONNECTED

- You make decisions together.
- You enjoy activities together.
- The needs of the family or the relationship come before the needs of individuals in the family.
- You and your partner work as a team.

EQUAL

- Each partner's needs are equally considered.
- The strengths of each partner are valued.
- Each partner is seen as intelligent and competent.
- The contributions of each partner are valued.

MUTUAL

- You share parenting and household responsibilities.
- You care for each other.
- You support each other's interests.
- You are respectful of each other.

Does this sound familiar to you? You have probably been approaching your relationship with the intention of being connected, equal, and mutual. It may be devastating for you to realize that you and your partner are working from two very different belief systems. You are working on creating a respectful and equal relationship. His primary concern has been with maintaining power and control and holding on to his superiority and privilege. You have been playing the game using different sets of rules and perhaps never knew it!

You have probably assumed that you and your partner share similar beliefs about your relationship—that you are both looking for connection, equality, and mutuality. While this is not true, what is true is that your partner assumes that you share his belief system. He believes you are also trying to be central, superior, and deserving. When you try to be part of the decision making, he thinks you are trying to take over. When you behave as his equal, he thinks you are trying to be better than he is. When you express your needs, he thinks you are being selfish. Abusive men often think that women are "out to get them" and sometimes act as though their partners are "the enemy." When men try to fight a war and women try to develop a relationship, women inevitably get hurt.

Your partner's belief system forces you into a lesser role. If your partner insists on being central, you are forced into being peripheral. If your partner believes he is superior, then you must be inferior. If your partner is deserving, then you end up serving his needs. His belief system drives you into this position. In order to protect yourself from further abuse, you are compelled to accommodate his desire to be central, superior, and deserving. We do not think you are "peripheral," "inferior," or "serving" but you have no choice. His dominant beliefs force you into this position in the relationship as you try to stay safe and avoid explosions.

DIAGRAM 7.2: ACCOMMODATING HIS DESIRE FOR CENTRALITY

YOUR PARTNER	YOU
Central	Peripheral
Superior	Inferior
Deserving	Serving

Sometimes women try to share this information with their partner, in the hope that he will change his behavior. However, your partner will likely disagree with the analysis. He will insist that he does not see himself as central, superior, and deserving, in part because these beliefs are usually held unconsciously by abusive men. The beliefs are deep-seated, and your partner may not be entirely aware of them. As well, it is unlikely that he would admit to such selfish attitudes. Abusive men will rarely say that they are the "center of the household" or "better than their partner" or "deserving of privileges." Their actions, however, betray their attitudes. If you want to test the theories of this chapter, we suggest you use your partner's behavior as evidence, rather than what he says he believes.

> *My partner always presented himself as being interested in "women's equality," and he "believed" he should do his share of housework. However, his behavior demonstrated a different set of beliefs. His constant criticisms pointed to his belief that he was superior to me. His disregard for my needs demonstrated his desire to be central and deserving. His actions were a better indication of his true belief system.*
>
> —GABRIELLE

IS IT POSSIBLE FOR ABUSIVE MEN TO CHANGE?

It is possible for abusive men to change. Now that you understand that your partner's abusiveness stems from his belief system, however, you can probably appreciate why change is very difficult. We are not talking about something relatively simple like managing his anger better or developing communication skills. If your partner is to truly change how he relates to you and your children, he will need to change his deep-seated beliefs about relationships.

You may be feeling like you want to talk to your partner about getting counseling but may not feel safe to approach him. If you know your partner will be explosive at the mention of counseling, you should listen to your inner voice and not bring it up. Some women will decide to talk to their partners about getting help for their abusiveness. If you do, here are some things to keep in mind. First, while you have a lot invested in his changing, you are not responsible for finding counseling or getting him help. If you do go so far as to find a good counseling program for him, once you have given him the contact information, it is his responsibility to follow up, attend, and work hard. It may be hard to step back and observe but your partner's actions will tell you a lot about his willingness to change.

Counseling for Abusive Men

It is very difficult for people to change their beliefs. It is especially difficult in this situation, because the belief system has been working well for your partner—he has been getting what he wants and has maintained his centrality, superiority, and deservedness.

In order to change, your partner has to want to change. He must acknowledge that the problem is abuse and that he is 100 percent responsible for the abuse. He has to register himself in counseling that holds men responsible for the abuse and then he has to work hard in his counseling program. He needs to work with a counselor who will challenge his basic ideas and assumptions about relationships. Ideally, he needs to participate in a counseling group for abusive men where he is held accountable for your safety and the safety of your children. He needs to demonstrate to you his willingness to be responsible and accountable for his behavior. The more accountability he has, the more likely he is to change and maintain those changes. If he is to change, it will take a long time.

Men who are abusive often resist counseling. They do not want to be challenged. Furthermore, most abusive men do not want others to know about their "bad" behavior. They want to keep their abuse a secret. Secrecy is part of what keeps the abuse working. If no one knows what your partner is doing to you, his actions have no consequences. It may be hard for you and your partner to imagine him taking part in a counseling program because his abusive behavior has been a secret for so long. But if your partner is to change, he needs to start being honest about what he is doing.

It is important to keep in mind that abusive men will sometimes use counseling as a tactic to regain control. Think back to the honeymoon phase of the Cycle of Abuse. Many women say that their partner promises to seek counseling during this phase. Some men actually follow through. Attending counseling, rather than just making promises, may be a first step for your partner. However, simply attending counseling will not be enough. He will need to commit to huge changes in order for you to feel safe. Your feeling safer is the only real indicator that he is starting to change.

If your partner refuses to go or clearly doesn't work hard in his counseling program, it is fair to assume that he will never stop his abusiveness. Even for men who are motivated and work hard, it is difficult to change such fundamental belief structures; it is unlikely your partner will change his beliefs on his own.

Anger Management Counseling

Some men who are abusive are referred to anger management programs. However, the problem is not your partner's anger but his underlying belief system. Therefore, it is unlikely that anger management will be beneficial. This can be difficult to understand at first. Your partner's anger is very threatening to you and may seem like the main problem, but it is not. Your partner's belief that he has a right to be central, superior, and deserving is the problem. When he feels these beliefs are being challenged, he may respond with anger.

It is also helpful to remember that anger is a tactic your partner uses to maintain power and control over you. His anger is intended to intimidate and silence you. Many women have reported to us that when their partner takes part in an anger management course, they do see some change in their partners' behavior. For example, they may stop hitting, yelling, or throwing things. But because the abusive belief system has not been challenged, these men simply use different tactics to maintain power and control. For example, they may escalate their emotional, sexual, or financial abuse. This dynamic can be very confusing for women. On the surface, it may seem like your partner is "getting better," but in fact, he has simply changed his tactics. Ultimately, his intention is to continue to control you.

Couple Counseling

You may have wondered if you and your partner should seek counseling together, or perhaps you've already tried this. Based on many women's experience, we advise against couple counseling for three reasons. First, with your partner present, it is unsafe for you to tell the counselor the truth of your relationship. If you do so, you will likely face the negative consequence of your partner's abuse sometime after the counseling as he tries to make you pay for what you said.

Second, if you are unable to be honest with the counselor because of your well-grounded fears, you are apt to give the counselor only a partial picture of your relationship. Your partner's behavior will not look as bad as it is. At the same time, your partner is likely to tell his worst stories about you. As a result, the counselor receives a very inaccurate picture of what's going on and is unhelpful in her or his advice. When abuse is involved, couple counseling is futile at its best and dangerous at its worst.

Third, the problem is your partner's. Couple counseling works when both people are responsible for the problems in the relationship and both want to work toward a solution. However, the abuse is solely your partner's responsibility, and he is the one who has to work at changing his behavior. After all the abuse has stopped, and you feel safe in expressing yourself, couple counseling may be an important step in establishing a respectful and trusting relationship. This can't happen, though, until you are safe to express yourself.

While your partner is going through counseling, we encourage you to seek a women's group for support. You may find the idea of group counseling with other women who have been abused a little intimidating. Perhaps you are influenced by the stereotype of "battered" women that exists in our society. Of all the hundreds of women we've had the pleasure to work with, none of them fit the stereotype—and all of them worried that they wouldn't fit into the group!

Whether your partner is in a counseling program or not, we encourage you to try attending a support group for women who experience abuse. After a few weeks, you'll know whether it is a group that is right for you. It is so much easier to deal with the impact of your partner's abuse with the support of other women who really understand what you have experienced.

WHAT CAN I EXPECT OF MY PARTNER?

Sometimes women who have been living with an abusive man for a long time feel that they no longer know what are reasonable expectations of their partner. We don't think this is true; we think you do know what is reasonable to expect in any relationship—respect, love, mutual support, safety, fun, etc. However, in an abusive relationship you can do little to have your expectations met. If you ask for them to be met, you will be accused of nagging. If you insist on them being met, you will be accused of being selfish or controlling. Your partner will become abusive, and you will be forced to back down. If you do not back down immediately, the abuse may escalate until you do. After many, many attempts, you have learned that it is futile to express your expectations. You may feel silenced or you may continue to try to express yourself. Either way, your opinions and needs are not valued by your partner.

In our counseling groups, we invite women to brainstorm about what they think are realistic expectations to have in a respectful relationship. We don't ask them to reflect on their own relationship, but rather on the ideas they have about relationships in general. They always come up with a lengthy and perfectly reasonable list. Here is a list from one group:

Reasonable Relationship Expectations

- ◯ Faithfulness
- ◯ Love
- ◯ Equality
- ◯ Loyalty
- ◯ Respect
- ◯ Trust
- ◯ Consideration
- ◯ Honesty
- ◯ Connectedness
- ◯ Sharing of responsibilities
- ◯ Concern for my well-being
- ◯ Acceptance of mistakes
- ◯ Support
- ◯ Valuing of family
- ◯ Shared decision making
- ◯ Dependability
- ◯ Humor
- ◯ Responsibility
- ◯ Sensitivity
- ◯ Encouragement
- ◯ Security (physical, emotional, financial)
- ◯ Being listened to
- ◯ Caring
- ◯ Being accepted without judgment
- ◯ Shared interests

When you look over this list, do you think it is a reasonable set of expectations for a respectful relationship? Are these the kinds of qualities that you try to offer in your relationship? In our experience, these are the qualities that make up a safe, healthy relationship, and women expect themselves to adhere to these values. If you are willing to bring these qualities to the relationship, it's reasonable to expect your partner to do the same.

If you were to review the list and ask yourself if your partner is meeting these expectations, how would this affect how you view your partner? It may be very painful to realize that your partner is not reciprocating even very basic expectations like trust, honesty, safety, and faithfulness.

We hope that the information in this chapter serves to fill in some missing pieces for you as you struggle to make sense of your partner's behavior. We realize that what you have read may be discouraging for you. Perhaps you didn't realize how vastly different you and your partner approach your relationship and how fundamentally he needs to change.

If your partner is really motivated to change, searches out a good counseling program for abusive men, and works hard in that program to ensure your safety, it is possible for him to change. You will know if the change is enough to meet your expectations for a respectful and loving relationship. Even if your partner is changing, you may not feel safe to engage again in the relationship. He may try to convince you of his changes. However, trust your inner voice and continue to look for evidence in his actions. Is he truly concerned about your well-being and safety? Even if he is changing, you may not feel safe or trust him enough to remain in a relationship with him. Sometimes trust is broken beyond repair.

If after reading this chapter, you worry that your partner will not change, it may be hard to know where to find hope. We encourage you to start placing hope in yourself rather than in your partner or the relationship. With the help of supportive people around you, you can start to envision a safer and better life. In Chapter 9, we will address how you can search out support for yourself. First, though, let's take a look at how your partner's abuse is affecting your children.

EIGHT

What's This Doing to My Kids?

I left my husband and got a place for my two-year-old daughter and myself. I hadn't realized how much my husband's abuse had negatively affected my daughter. In our new apartment she could make noise. She would sing and yell and dance around the house. It was wonderful to see. She finally felt safe to be herself.

—DIANE

HOW IS MY PARTNER'S ABUSE IMPACTING MY CHILDREN?

The abuse he was doing toward our son was heartbreaking. The last thing he said to him before we went to the shelter was, "I wish I could smack you upside your head, but I know I can't because I'd get into trouble."

—DANICA

You may worry about how your children are being affected by your partner's abuse. Perhaps you are concerned that your children are learning from your partner's behavior. You may be fearful that your children will grow up to be abusive or to be abused. You may feel that you are not a good enough mother. We understand your concern. Every woman we know struggles with trying to be a good mom. Mothering is hard work, but mothering is especially difficult if you have a partner that is undermining you and creating stress for you and your children. We hope this chapter will help to make sense of the concerns you have as a mother and help you to see all the ways you have been supporting your kids.

Women often ask how their children are being affected by the abuse. This is a difficult question to ask, and it takes a lot of courage to explore this. It can be very painful to look at how your partner's abuse is affecting your children. If your children are witnessing or overhearing the explosions, you are probably aware of how this is impacting your children. But even if the explosions happen only when the children are not around, your partner uses many tactics of abuse that can also affect them. Your children may be demonstrating behaviors that are worrisome such as having nightmares, not sleeping well, overeating, struggling with school, or showing signs of depression or anxiety. Think back to the impact list in Chapter 5. Your children can experience impacts similar to yours, no matter how much you have tried to protect them from your partner's abuse.

Your partner's behavior can be confusing and frightening for your children. Maybe he has inconsistent consequences for your children, which can be stressful. Perhaps he has unrealistic expectations of your children, making them feel that they are never good enough. Maybe he spends time with them one day, then refuses to be with them for long periods of time. Maybe he appears to be an involved father on the soccer field but ignores them at home. Perhaps he is harsher with one child and gives preferential treatment to another. This is likely very hard for you, as your voice does not make a difference in how he treats your children.

Sometimes women tell us that their partner is a "good dad," at least some of the time. Maybe he buys the kids gifts or sometimes takes them fun places. But other times he may disregard the kids or be hurtful with his words or actions. This lack of consistency is really hard for children and for you. Think back to the Cycle of Abuse in Chapter 2. Your partner may use the children in different ways throughout the Cycle. This is confusing for the children and for you. He may seem like a good dad some days and a terrible dad other days depending on the phase of the Cycle he is in. But remember, good parents do not manipulate or control their children, nor do they parent only when it is convenient for them. They try to be consistent with their children and work hard to meet their children's needs.

> *I used to tell everyone that Pavil was a great dad and I used to think he was, but now I see things differently. Pavil would play with the kids when it suited him, but it always had to fit with his timing and be on his terms. If things got hard or messy with the kids, he was nowhere to be found. I was the one making the lunches for school every day.*
>
> —DAGMARA

Even if your partner does treat the children well most of the time, if he abuses you, he is not a good dad. Part of the definition of a "good dad" is that he treats you (the mom) with care and respect.

Because children do not have the same tools and abilities you have for expressing confusion or hurt over how your partner's abuse is affecting them, they may end up expressing themselves in ways that are troubling for you. Their behavior may become quite concerning to you as a mother, whether they are turning their anger on you, expressing hopelessness, or telling you they want to hurt themselves or someone else. Maybe they have been labeled a bully at school, or maybe they are the victims of bullying. It is awful to feel that your children are suffering because of your partner's behaviors.

You may wonder if your children's behavior is a result of being exposed to your partner's abuse or if it is normal childhood behavior. If, for example, your teenage son suddenly becomes quite rude or disrespectful to you, you may struggle to determine whether he is imitating his father or whether he is just trying to assert normal teenage independence. First of all, it might be helpful to realize that many parents struggle to make sense of their children's behaviors. However, if you are concerned about your child's behavior, we encourage you to pay attention to it. Do not disregard it because of the abuse.

The good news is that, even though you are concerned about your child's safety and development, research shows that having one safe parent that is nurturing and caring is very important for a child to grow up to be an emotionally healthy person. Of course you are concerned about the negative influence of your partner on your kids, but we hope that you will be able to see more clearly the essential and positive role you play in your child's life.

HOW HAS MY PARTNER'S ABUSE IMPACTED MY ABILITY TO MOTHER?

Not only does your partner's abuse affect your children, but it is probably having an impact on how you mother them. Living with an abusive man can severely hamper your ability to be the mother you want to be. Your partner might control or prevent you from parenting your children the way you feel is appropriate. Perhaps when you try to parent in a way that seems loving and supportive, your partner undermines you by telling your children to ignore you. The way that he monitors your interactions with your children might put tremendous pressure on you and make you feel you can never meet his expectations. Or maybe he belittles you in front of the children. If your abusive partner sees the children as interfering with his relationship with you, you may feel unsafe to express love and affection toward your children. Perhaps the fear created by your partner's unpredictable and erratic behavior interferes with you caring for your children because you are forced to focus on his behavior. Your focus on staying safe might get more of your attention and leave less time and attention for your kids.

Not only do women have serious concerns about how their partner's abuse is affecting their children, but they also worry that they are either "too hard on" or "too lenient with" their children. Some of this is the uncertainty created by the Cycle of Abuse, whereby your partner will tell you what a wonderful mother you are one day and then be very critical of your parenting the next. If you have yelled at or hit your children, you may have worried about becoming abusive yourself. Your partner's abuse leaves you exhausted and tense. Because of this, you may feel that you are not always the mother you want to be.

On the other hand, some women find that they are too lenient or indulgent with their children. Maybe your children behave rudely or inappropriately, and you don't correct them because you want them to feel safe with you. If this is what is happening in your situation, you may have realized that you are "easy" on your children in order to compensate for your partner's abuse. You feel that your partner is always giving your children a hard time so you want to give them a break. He may undermine you or tell the children they can disregard what you have said, or yell at the kids for not "obeying" you. You may also find that if you try to correct or teach your children, your partner will step in and sabotage your efforts.

I get stressed out anytime I have to tell the kids to do anything because I worry about my partner jumping in and taking over. He will yell at them and shame them. I just wanted to give them some direction. I can't say what I want to say to the kids because my partner will overreact and explode. Then I find myself protecting the kids from his reaction rather than delivering a parenting message.

—PRIYA

It is heartbreaking that you can't follow your own mothering instincts without interference or fear, but we are always impressed with the care that women give to their children in such a challenging and unpredictable context. We want you to recognize the ways that you have protected your children from your partner's negative behaviors.

It seems to us that mothers are held to a much higher parenting standard than dads. We have noticed that women seem to have to prove their ability to parent their children whereas men do not have to defend their parenting. Perhaps you have felt judged because you are often exhausted by the abuse and therefore not always at your best as a mom. You are juggling so much—all the regular demands of parenting plus the undermining and sabotaging from your partner. While you are working hard to protect your children, your partner's public displays of parenting bring him lots of recognition as a "good dad." It might even feel that people are siding with your partner and feel he is the "better" parent. We understand this terrible dilemma—people do not see what you are living with and how hard you have to work to keep you and your children safe.

Jason had been awful all weekend. He kept going on rages about the state of the house. I was trying to keep the kids out of his way and get the house tidied up at the same time. My nerves were shot.

Sunday night his mom and dad came for dinner. I had done every-thing to get the house ready, the food prepared, and the kids cleaned up. With his folks here, he got down on the floor and played with the kids. His mom turned to me and said, "He's such a good dad, isn't he?" I thought, "All he has to do is play for a few minutes and he's a 'good dad'?"

—REBA

As we think about some of the ways that your partner's abuse impacts your ability to mother, it might be helpful to think back to the Power and Control Wheel in Chapter 4. In that chapter, we talked about some of the tactics your partner uses to control you through the children. The following is an expanded list of some of these tactics:

○ Belittling me in front of the children
○ Using the children to his advantage
○ Telling me I'm a terrible mother
○ Telling the children I'm a terrible mother
○ Lying to the children
○ Lying to the children about me
○ Threatening to harm the children
○ Harming the children
○ Claiming that the children's bad behavior is the reason for his violence

○ Encouraging the children to abuse me
○ Threatening violence against the children and/or their pets
○ Engaging the children in a negative discussion about me
○ Threatening to take the children from me
○ Threatening a long court battle for custody, even though he has shown little interest in the children

This list may be overwhelming to look at. It is very painful to realize that your partner seems to be willing to use the children to meet his own needs for power and control. You probably work very hard to try to protect your children from harm. It can be shocking to realize that your partner may intentionally be harming the children to maintain his position of power. His behaviors create fear and confusion in your family. In the process of harming you, he harms the children. He seems to be willing to use the children as pawns in the very damaging game he is playing with your life.

Despite your partner's treatment of you and your children, you have been doing many things to protect and care for your children.

> *He was very abusive, and he was directing some of it at our son. He would call him terrible, hurtful names. I would always get in the way and separate them. I didn't care what happened to me.*
>
> —JOSIE

The woman in the quote above describes the lengths she would go to in order to protect her children, including risking her own safety. Let's look at some of the positive things you are already doing to care for and support your children.

Here is a list of some examples from other women:

I spend extra time one-on-one with my kids.

I make a point of affirming the good I see in them.

After an explosion from my partner, I say to them, "That was wrong."

I take them out of the house and away from him.

I try to bring other good people into their lives.

I spend extra time with my child at bedtime—lots of books and cuddles.

I keep information about the kids from my partner to avoid an explosion.

I take my kids to my parents' when my partner is escalating.

I stay involved with their teachers.

I make sure I make good meals for the kids.

You can probably think of many things you do to ensure that your children feel safe and cared for. Maybe you would like to write down a few of these things.

_____

_____

_____

_____

WHY DO MY CHILDREN "SIDE" WITH THEIR FATHER?

Despite women's efforts to protect and care for their children, many women are confused by their children's behavior toward their father. Children will sometimes appear to prefer their father to their mother and may even defend their father's abusive actions. This can be a very painful and confusing experience. We assume that children will feel more connected with the safe and dependable parent, but it is precisely because you are safe and dependable that your children can act out against you. Because your partner's behavior is unpredictable and frightening, your children are less likely to do anything to upset him. You become the parent who can be tested and pushed. The testing of parents is part of normal childhood development, but you are the only parent with whom it is safe to do so.

Your children may also feel that it is necessary to "take sides" in the war your partner is creating. Your partner is the powerful and unsafe one in your relationship. Aligning themselves with the person who has power is a wise thing for your children to do. It helps keep your children safe, and your children may think it helps to keep you safe, too.

Recognizing that your children are doing this as part of the impact of abuse may allow for a helpful shift in your thinking. It may help you to be clear about who is to blame for your children acting out. Your children are doing the best they can in the impossible situation your partner is creating. The more you can have compassion for your children, the more likely you will be able to be emotionally available and present for them. Here are some quotes that we think illustrate this shift in thinking.

I realize now that my daughter is burdened by his anger. She is forced to carry his anger.

—SYDNEY

When my son is hostile toward me, I look for the crack in his armor where I can come in with love. I ignore as much as possible the angry behavior, and when we do connect with each other, I make the most

of it. The other day he showed me something really funny on YouTube.
We laughed and laughed. It felt healing.

—POLLY

When my kids are spinning off with bad behavior, I try to help them
calm down. I get them something to eat, I put them in the bath, and
I say to myself, "They are overwhelmed. They need help."

—GEORGIA

When my daughter attacks me with hurtful words that I know come
from her dad, I try to remember that we are both *under attack. She*
is saying the words, but they come from him.

—KIM

Parenting children within the context of abuse is difficult. You
deserve as much good support as you can find. Try to take comfort
in knowing that your children are acting up with you because you
are the safe parent to act up with. You make your children feel safe
and secure. That is good.

HOW CAN I TALK TO MY CHILDREN ABOUT THIS?

Women struggle with what to say to their children about their partner's abuse. They do not want to sabotage their children's relationship
with their father. At the same time, they see their children being
hurt and want to protect them from this pain. It becomes a balanc-
ing act: How can you teach your children about abuse without
sounding like you are being unfair to their father?

Remind yourself that if your partner is being abusive, *he* is the
one sabotaging his relationship with his children. His selfishness

and abuse have hurt you, the children, and the stability of your family. These are all consequences of his actions, not yours. If you speak to your children about the abuse, remember that you are only helping them to understand what your partner is doing. Your partner's behavior is the problem, and not your speaking about it. You want to be sure not to minimize or dismiss the abuse, as this would be confusing for your child.

It may also be helpful to separate the abusive behavior from your partner himself. When talking to your child, try to focus on your partner's behavior, not on him as a person. Talk about specific situations as abusive or hurtful. For example, you could say, "It was wrong when your dad yelled at you for spilling the milk," instead of saying, "Your dad was a real jerk about the spilled milk." Try to speak to your children when you are not too upset yourself. If you are feeling overwhelmed with emotion, you will not likely communicate at your best. Give yourself some time to cool down and speak to your children when you have a few quiet moments with them. Try to put yourself in their situation and think about what is helpful for them to hear from you or talk about with you. For example, you do not need to burden them with your fears, but it would be very helpful to listen to their feelings and fears with as much composure as you can gather. You might also say to your children that people should not feel afraid of anyone in their families, and if someone makes them feel afraid, it is not their fault.

Most research in this area shows that children are far more aware of the abuse than their mothers realize. You may be avoiding this conversation because you think it will be upsetting for your children. However, most children know things are not okay, but do not have the vocabulary to describe what is really going on. If your children know that they can speak to you about the abuse, they will be less afraid. Things will seem a little less out of control. Your children may also let go of the feeling that they are responsible for the abuse or for stopping it. Just like you, it is important that children hear that they are not responsible or to blame for the abuse. And that they can't do anything to prevent your partner's behavior.

WILL MY CHILDREN GROW UP TO ABUSE OR BE ABUSED?

If your children witness your partner's abuse, you are probably concerned about what they are learning. You may worry that your son will grow up to be abusive or that your daughter will think abuse is "normal" and marry an abusive man. While it is true that your partner's abuse is impacting your children, it is not true that they are destined to live in abusive relationships the rest of their lives. You can do a number of things to help your children learn about respectful behavior.

First, talk to your children about abusive and respectful behavior. As much as possible, teach your children the vocabulary necessary to describe what is acceptable and appropriate versus disrespectful and abusive. Some women find it helpful to talk about abuse in terms of bullying. Your children are likely learning about bullying in school. You can say, "It is not okay to be a bully in school; it is not okay to be a bully at home." If it is difficult to talk about your partner's behavior, use others as material for discussion. Talk about behavior you see in the mall or on television. If some behavior is abusive, call it that. If you experience kind and respectful behavior, comment on it. Try to talk about all the different kinds of abuse. Be sure that your children know about verbal and emotional abuse and not just physical abuse. If you are not living with your partner, and if your children are old enough, you may be able to draw a

Power and Control Wheel with them (see Chapter 4). Have your children identify the different types of abuse they have witnessed or experienced. If you give your children the vocabulary to understand abusive behavior, they are then able to draw their own conclusions about their father's behavior.

Remember that people who were raised in abusive homes can and do choose to live in a different way as adults. If you give your children the vocabulary they need for understanding abuse and its effects on others, you will help them to choose to live free of abuse. You can also help your children develop empathy by talking about how disrespectful or bullying behaviors feel—the impacts of abuse. As we learned in Chapter 7, something that abusive men are lacking is the ability to see how their abusive behaviors are affecting their partners and their children.

Second, consider nurturing relationships with people who are positive role models for your children. Do you know men who treat others in respectful, loving ways? Perhaps your children have a grandfather, an uncle, or a family friend who could spend more time with them. Hopefully teachers and coaches will also serve as good role models. We realize your partner may sabotage efforts to provide your children with good role models and isolate you and your children from people outside your home. However, if this is not the case, take some comfort in realizing that your partner is not your children's only model of how to relate to others.

Third, you may consider leaving. Attempting to limit the amount of abuse your children witness is a way to minimize the negative impact your partner is having on them. We recognize that this is a difficult option to consider, and we would like to explore this below and in more detail in Chapter 10. First, let's look at how to get support for you and your children.

HOW DO I GET SUPPORT AS A MOTHER?

It is extremely challenging to mother in the context of abuse. We would encourage you to draw on any support you can. You may find it helpful to speak with other parents about your children's behavior. Nurture friendships with parents of similarly aged children. In a sense, you really do not have a "co-parent" in your partner. It may be more accurate to say that your partner is actively sabotaging your parenting. Getting support from other parents may help you feel less alone and give you a sounding board for your concerns.

You may also want to do some reading. The library and the Internet can be great resources. Remember, however, that because your partner is abusive, some advice in books or on the Internet may not apply to your situation. For example, some books may suggest that your partner is trying to have a healthy attachment with your child, but this may not be true. These are some books we recommend: *When Dad Hurts Mom* by Lundy Bancroft, *How to Co-Parent with an Abusive Ex and Keep Your Sanity* by Julie Boyd Cole, and *Divorce Poison* by Dr. Richard Warshak.

Finally, if you are concerned about how the abuse is affecting your children, you could consider getting them appropriate counseling. Many communities have programs designed for children who have witnessed or been exposed to violence or abuse in their homes. Such counseling will give your children a safe environment to talk about what is going on in their life. Specially trained counselors who are knowledgeable about the impacts of abuse are a good source of support for both you and your children. You can find out if your community has this form of counseling by calling a women's shelter or women's resource center.

STAYING OR LEAVING?
WHAT'S BEST FOR MY CHILDREN?

Often women who are dealing with an abusive partner find themselves severely limited when it comes to providing what is best for their children. For example, women sometimes stay in relationships where they are being abused because they are financially dependent on their partners. If a woman stays with her partner, the children may continue to witness the abuse. If she leaves, she and her children might struggle financially. Unfortunately, abusive men will go to great lengths to avoid paying child support, even if the court has ordered it. In such situations women are left with limited options—and none of them are what you want for you and your children. This feels really unfair!

Another dilemma women find themselves in is attempting to protect their children from their father's behavior. You may have felt pressure from yourself, from friends or family, or from professionals to remove your children from your partner's abuse. However, you may have found that your ability to do so is quite limited. Courts will protect a father's "right" to have access to his children. Again women find themselves in a challenging situation. If you stay with your partner, you are accused of not shielding your children from abuse. However, if you leave, the courts will likely give your partner access to your children. More and more it seems that the courts are giving shared custody to separated parents, even in situations where the father has been abusive to the mother. The current legal climate seems to put fathers' rights above the safety of women and children. You are caught in a seemingly impossible situation. You want to protect your children and society expects you to protect them, but at the same time, the legal system protects your partner's "rights" to be with them.

We have outlined these two difficult scenarios not in order to discourage you. We simply hope to identify some of the struggles and dilemmas you may be facing. We also hope to help you to see that the limitations you are experiencing when it comes to providing what is best for your children have more to do with our legal and social systems than they do with your ability as a parent. As a society, we need to ensure that fathers pay child support and that children are protected from witnessing or experiencing abuse. Until we do, however, women like you are forced to work within limited options. It is possible, with good support and legal advice, to make life for your children safer and better, but it may well be a struggle and you may continue to encounter roadblocks to doing what you know is best. It will be helpful for you to learn as much as you can about the law and understand your rights. Women's shelters and women's resource centers can provide support and often have a list of lawyers that are accustomed to supporting women and their children through the legal process. They may also have suggestions about free legal resources in your community.

Trying to protect your children and navigate the legal system while your partner continues to be abusive can be overwhelming and exhausting. You have been and continue to be the primary person looking out for your children's best interest. Your partner is not doing this. He is engaging the legal process with the intention of "winning" by maintaining power and control but he will likely present himself as very concerned about the children. You may be the only person who understands his true motives. We want you to know that what you are doing shows great courage and strength.

In this chapter, we have tried to address the concerns you have when it comes to your partner's impact on your children. Because of your partner's abuse, you are forced to carry a lot of responsibility, but sometimes it feels like an impossible responsibility. As much as you try to protect and parent your children, your partner's abuse overrides your best intentions. You have lots of evidence to suggest that your partner will not put the physical and emotional needs of his children before his own needs. This leaves you to look out for their interests. As well, you know from experience that there are limits put on you when it comes to doing what is best for your children—limits imposed by your partner, his abusive behavior, or the courts. Nevertheless, we hope that through this chapter we have affirmed what you are already doing for your children as well as given you some ideas of things you might do in the future to support them and to get support for them from the community. However, it is not only your children who need and deserve support right now. You do, too. Our next chapter will look at ways to get the help you need.

NINE

Am I Getting the Support I Need?

I needed to tell someone. I needed support from people who would be concerned for my safety and well-being. A friend referred me to a counseling agency. I joined a support group for women. The first few weeks of group counseling were wonderful for me. I began to understand how so much of Peter's behavior toward me was abusive. I discovered that I didn't deserve to be treated that way by my partner. I discovered I was not crazy. And I discovered I was not alone.

—MARION

HOW DO I KNOW IF I'M GETTING THE RIGHT SUPPORT?

This book has taken you through a difficult journey, exploring your relationship from the perspective of inequality and abuse. We have looked at how your partner's abuse has had far-reaching implications for you and has affected many aspects of your life. Because his abuse has likely affected you mentally, emotionally, physically, spiritually, and financially, you may need to draw on a range of supportive services such as emergency housing for women, police, legal services, health services, social services, and counseling in order to deal with all the impacts of the abuse. In this chapter we will review what supports you may already be leaning on and help you identify what additional supports might be helpful. We will also evaluate with you what makes for a helpful support person and what kind of support can actually make your situation worse.

While there are many good services to support women who have experienced abuse, unfortunately not all sources of support are helpful. Sometimes women are given dangerous advice (for example, therapists may tell women to stand up to their partners, when it is not safe to do so). Sometimes police don't show up when they're called, and sometimes social service workers treat women disrespectfully.

Hopefully you have some positive support in your life, but many women tell us that they have encountered both helpful and unhelpful supports as well as other barriers to services. In the exercise below, we will help you to assess your current supports. Let's start by talking about some criteria for evaluating a source of support:

1. Do they believe me 100 percent of the time?
2. Are they concerned about my emotional and physical well-being more than they are concerned about my partner or the relationship?
3. Do they understand the dynamics of abuse and that there are many different forms of abuse?
4. Are they trustworthy and respectful? Do I know that they will respect the confidentiality of what I tell them?
5. Do they emphasize my strengths and affirm me?
6. Are they dependable? Can I rely on them to be reasonably available when I need them?
7. Can I access the service? (Do I have the money? Can I get to it? Is there a waiting list?)

Other criteria for good support:

_____

_____

_____

_____

In the exercise on the next page, we have listed some potential sources of support. Place a checkmark in the box beside the person or service if this is a positive source of support for you. Place an X in the box if your experience with this person or service has been negative. Leave the box blank if you have had no contact with this person or service. Next, beside each person or service, make a few notes about how or why this person or service has been helpful or unhelpful for you. We have noticed that some women have a positive experience with one person in an organization and a negative experience with another person within the same organization. If this is true for you, you can also note that.

Here is an example to illustrate how to complete the exercise:

Jane reports that her doctor does not listen well and jumps in too quickly with simple solutions. She is reluctant to share information with her doctor. Celia finds her doctor to be very supportive, a good listener, and genuinely concerned about her mental and physical well-being.

Jane would put an X beside "Doctor" while Celia would likely give her doctor a checkmark. Jane might comment that her doctor did not take her seriously and thought her problems were

Evaluating Your Support

POTENTIAL SOURCES OF SUPPORT	HOW HAS THIS PERSON OR SERVICE BEEN HELPFUL OR UNHELPFUL?
☐ Women's shelter or safe housing	
☐ Victim services	
☐ Women's resource center	
☐ Group counseling for women	
☐ Counselors for you or for your children	
☐ Family	
☐ Friends	
☐ Immigrant support services	
☐ Doctor or health-care provider	
☐ Mental health services	
☐ Addiction services	
☐ Lawyer	
☐ Police	
☐ Employment (boss/co-workers)	
☐ Employment training	
☐ Child care	
☐ Children's school	
☐ Recreation center, social or sports club	

continues on next page . . .

POTENTIAL SOURCES OF SUPPORT	HOW HAS THIS PERSON OR SERVICE BEEN HELPFUL OR UNHELPFUL?
☐ Social services/social worker	
☐ Food bank	
☐ Church/faith community	
☐ Spiritual leader	
☐ _____	
☐ _____	
☐ _____	

insignificant, while Celia might say that her doctor makes her feel believed and deserving of support.

We invite you to take some time to review this list of possible sources of support. Make some notes about whether each source of support has, in fact, been helpful or unhelpful to you. Ask yourself how each of these people or places makes you feel about yourself and the challenges you are facing. Are there barriers such as waiting lists, disrespectful staff, or lack of child care that prevent you from accessing or returning to a support?

Now that you have considered the above list, we suggest that you go back and put a star beside those people and services that consistently give you positive and dependable support. Take note of how many stars you have. You may have only a couple stars, or perhaps none. This is not uncommon; it is hard to find good, reliable support. Maybe this is a good time to try to expand your support network. Are there people or services on the list that you could consider reaching out to? We know that it is hard to reach out. There are many barriers that prevent women from accessing the supports they need. The next section will explore some of these barriers.

WHAT ARE THE BARRIERS TO MY GETTING SUPPORT?

Working on the above exercise, you may have noticed that you have encountered barriers to getting positive support. You are not alone in encountering barriers to good support. Sometimes barriers to service come from limits imposed by a partner. If a woman's partner limits her access to the phone, car, child care, or money, it is difficult to access some services. Some women can't afford to speak to a lawyer or can't get the car to visit a friend. Abusive men also use threats to try to limit their partner's access to services, such as the police. Maybe your partner insists on accompanying you to all your appointments so you cannot be honest about what is happening to you.

> *I was seeing my doctor because of depression. The main reason I was depressed was my partner's abuse but my partner came to all my appointments with me. He wouldn't let me go by myself. He acted very concerned with the doctor. He always came with me so I could never say what was actually going on.*
>
> —JULIET

Some services are difficult to access. Women may face long waiting lists for support groups, employment training, or counseling for their children. Sometimes they do not qualify for the service that they need (e.g., legal aid). Sometimes women feel so poorly treated that they will not return to that person or service.

Other barriers to accessing these services have to do with the fear of the unknown. For example, thinking about going to a women's shelter or safe house for the first time can be very intimidating. Everyone is anxious when going to a place for the first time, but women often find safety and support at a women's shelter and so it may be worth reaching out to this service even though it feels frightening. Another barrier to support might be that you feel like you don't "fit the stereotype" and therefore don't qualify for the service. For example, women who haven't been physically abused often think they do not qualify for a women's shelter or counseling for "battered" women.

If you are exhausted because of the abuse, embarrassed by your situation, or have had bad experiences with some institutions in the past, these can be barriers that prevent you from reaching out for help. Some women tell us they feel ashamed of what is going on in their home and this keeps them silent. Sometimes women say, "I feel shame that I 'allowed' the abuse to happen." Hopefully by now you see that you are not "allowing" anything to happen; in fact, you are resisting his abuse in many ways. Sometimes women don't reach out because they don't want to bring shame on their partner, but speaking the truth is not bringing shame on him. It is his actions that are shameful, not you talking about them.

Reaching out for support can also be confusing. You may feel like you are being bounced from service to service, or are being shuffled around without being listened to or having your needs met. It is not easy to navigate the many services that you will need to assist you and your children. It can all be very frustrating, jumping through hoops to meet the criteria for a program only to find out that there is a four-month waiting list. You may feel overwhelmed with dealing with the legal system, welfare system, children's services, or mental health services. You probably never imagined that you would have to make use of some of these services. What you are trying to sort through is too much for one person to do alone. You should not be alone. We know it is hard, people may let you down or "not get it," but we encourage you to persist in seeking good support because you are so deserving of it.

WHY IS IT SO HARD TO GET GOOD SUPPORT?

Women often find only a few sources of support, and some services or individuals who attempt to be supportive turn out to be disappointing or may even make matters worse. Here are some examples:

YAN WHA

Yan Wha finally gets up the courage to call the police after one of her husband's physical assaults. When the police question her, she feels she's being interrogated. When she has no physical evidence to show them, they grow skeptical. She asks them to remove her husband from the home. After speaking with him, however, they clearly accept his version of the story and do not remove him. The police should have believed Yan Wha and been concerned for her safety. They should have either removed her partner or taken her to a safe place.

BETH

After a night of relentless emotional abuse, Beth goes to see her pastor. For the first time, she really reveals how terrible her family situation is for her. Her pastor seems genuinely concerned and she finds herself telling him more than she intended. The pastor promises to be helpful to Beth and says a prayer with her. Beth leaves the office feeling better. She is shocked, however, when her husband comes home early from work, in a rage. The pastor had stopped by his work and confronted him about his behavior in the marriage. Although Beth did not think to state her need for confidentiality, her pastor should have assumed it. Although her pastor's actions were well intentioned, they put Beth at risk.

SARAH

Sarah is living with her husband and is beginning to consider a separation. She decides to see a counselor for support and for help in sorting through her complex situation. She goes to a counselor who has been highly recommended by a friend. The counselor tells her that he would like to see her and her husband together. What follows is a series of marriage counseling sessions with the goal of mending the relationship. Sarah is given a lot of advice for dealing with the conflict and anger in her relationship. The therapist tells Sarah that relationship conflict is normal and that it is important for her to hear her partner's anger without retreating. The counselor suggests that her inability to deal with her partner's anger stems from her father's anger.

Sarah knows from experience that asserting herself puts her at risk of a verbal or physical assault from her partner. Furthermore, the counselor's focus on Sarah as the one with "the problem" does not affirm or strengthen her. Finally, the suggestion that the problem is anger rather than abuse makes the impact of abuse invisible.

These examples are not intended to discourage you but to make one simple point: If you have not received the support you need, it is not your fault. It can be difficult to find good support. It may be helpful to broaden your sources of support, although this can be difficult. You know that it can be risky to tell someone about your situation. You don't know if they will believe you and you may wonder if they are dependable and trustworthy.

Unfortunately, you need to be a wise consumer when it comes to support. If a salesperson at your local store were rude to you, you would likely shop somewhere else next time. Similarly, if someone who is supposed to be supporting you is not, it is okay to look elsewhere for the support you deserve.

We realize how difficult this is. It is much more difficult to change your doctor or your faith community than it is to change shopping patterns. However, it will ultimately be more helpful to you if you're able to find some true support for yourself. We also realize that we are sometimes stuck with people or services. For example, your boss may be completely unsympathetic to your situation, but you may not be in a position to change jobs. Of course, you also have no control over who makes up your family. You can't trade your parents or siblings for ones that might be more understanding or supportive. If you realize how supportive or unsupportive these nonnegotiable people are, you can then be realistic about the role they will play in your life at this time. If your boss is unsupportive, don't look to him or her for support. Perhaps a co-worker will provide better support. If your siblings continue to be critical of you, you may choose to spend less time with them, at least for now. You are in a difficult time in your life. Try not to waste your limited energy on people who are unable or unwilling to support you.

HOW DO I FIND GOOD SUPPORT?

Although it is difficult to find good support, it is certainly not impossible. Having worked in this field for many years, we have met amazing service providers who care deeply about women and understand abuse. There are great people out there who get it and want to support you. Just because you have had a bad experience with one or more service providers, please do not give up.

SIERRA

Sierra is staying at a women's shelter and needs temporary financial support for her and her three children. When she meets with the welfare worker and explains her situation, she is shocked by how rude and abusive the worker is. She is asked many probing and embarrassing questions and leaves feeling judged and ashamed. She feels uncertain as to whether she will receive any actual help and is worried she will be forced to return to her partner. Fortunately for Sierra, when she returns to the women's shelter and tells her advocate about her experience at the welfare office, the advocate assures her that she will accompany her to her next appointment. Sierra feels relieved about this and is grateful to have this support. She does not want to deal with this disrespectful worker on her own.

Finding the right service or person to help make sense of your situation and advocate for you can be very helpful. Sierra is fortunate to be staying at a women's shelter, but even if you don't plan to stay at a shelter, you can often use their services. You can call them for suggestions about counseling programs, support groups, children's support, lawyers, and dealing with social services. You can also call your local women's resource center or the YWCA. If you do not know the phone number of your closest shelter or safe house, consider calling the crisis line in your community and ask them for the phone number.

Attending a women's support group and connecting with women who have had similar experiences can be an invaluable resource for you. Women who have attended our "When Love Hurts Support Groups" tell us that they were really nervous on the first night of group. Women worry that they won't fit in or that they will be too nervous to talk. But by the end of group, women tell us how much they love the support and care they receive. Some women describe the support group as a "lifeline" for them. Support groups help women realize that they are not alone, they are not crazy, and they are not responsible for the abuse. You can find out if there is a support group for women who have experienced abuse in your community by talking to your women's shelter or resource center. It is truly wonderful to be part of a support group.

You may find that the services you seek are described as being for "battered women," "domestic abuse," or "family violence." We know that all these names suggest physical violence and this may not be your experience, but professionals who work in the field of woman abuse understand that there are many different forms of abuse and they should take all forms seriously.

The Internet can also be a good source for information. If you are using a computer or mobile device that your partner has access to, please be diligent about deleting or hiding your history. Some women choose to use a friend's computer or a computer at a public library so they know their partner has no way of seeing their search history. We would encourage you to look at our website, which is WhenLoveHurts.ca. We have posted lots of helpful articles, videos, and resources. We have also posted information that might be helpful for family, friends, or other support people.

Sometimes women who have experienced abuse also struggle with substance abuse or mental health concerns. If this is true for you, you may experience even more barriers to finding good support. For example, some programs tell women that they must "deal with their addiction" before they can access services. As we found in Chapter 4, there is a connection between living through the effects of abuse and developing substance use or mental health concerns. Many women who have experienced mental health problems such as depression or anxiety report that these conditions were a result of the abuse they experienced. As one woman said, "Some people call it mental ill health. I call it symptoms of abuse." If you had mental health concerns before your relationship began, you may have noticed that these symptoms have worsened because of the abuse.

Similarly, there is a link between abuse and substance use. Perhaps you drink or use substances to numb the pain of the abuse or escape the constant fear and dread associated with the relationship. An abusive partner may also coerce or force you to use substances with him, and this might be safer for you than resisting. Whatever your reasons, it is important to know that you are coping the best you can.

Unfortunately, not all service providers have made this connection, which makes services less accessible for you. You may be afraid to tell someone about your struggles with substances or the mental health impacts of abuse because you fear that your children will be taken away from you. You may also have been made to feel ashamed for using street or prescription drugs to cope. Take heart. It may take some work to find an organization or person that sees the links between substance use, mental health, and experiences of abuse, but it is possible.

Women often want to gather legal information in order to protect themselves and their children should they decide to leave at some point. Friends or family members may give you advice, but remember the law is very complicated. Well-meaning people sometimes give faulty information. As well, your partner may have intimidated you with legal threats that you will want to check out with an expert. It is very important for you to know your legal rights, especially when children are involved. You can access legal information by calling Legal Aid or Legal Services or searching the Internet for local legal clinics that offer free advice.

HOW CAN I PLAN AHEAD?

It may be difficult to plan for the future. Part of the struggle may be that your partner's abuse leaves you exhausted and off balance. Because of this, it may be difficult to do more than just get through the day. For some women, the physical, financial, or social threats their partners throw at them keep them from making plans for the future. We recognize all these barriers and understand what a paralyzing effect they may have on you.

We would, however, encourage you to do as much thinking about the future as you are able. It may be difficult right now to contemplate leaving your home, but this need may arise at some point. It is much more difficult to think about what you should do when you are in the middle of a crisis than if you have a plan in place ahead of time. Remind yourself that just because you have a plan, it doesn't mean you have to use it. For example, you can say to yourself, "If I had to leave, this is where I would go."

You may also be thinking about separating from your partner permanently. Often this seems completely overwhelming. Breaking a seemingly overwhelming problem into smaller, attainable steps is a good idea. Start by gathering resources and information for yourself. For example, going to a lawyer and seeking advice about protecting your children and your financial security can be an important early step. It would be wise not to tell your partner if you see a lawyer. Even though it may seem deceptive to keep this information from him, remember that your partner's belief structure permits him to put his needs and desires before yours or your children's (see Chapter 7). In the event of a separation, his main concern will be his own well-being. Unfortunately, that leaves only you to be concerned about yourself and your children. Consulting a lawyer is an important step in protecting yourself and them.

Every woman is in a unique situation and has different things to consider as she thinks about her future. For this reason, we have included some concrete ideas about planning in different situations. Please look at these ideas and decide what fits your experience.

IF YOU ARE LIVING WITH YOUR PARTNER

- Decide where you will go if you have to leave home, even if you don't think you will have to. Where would you go if your first choice didn't work out?
- Know how to exit safely. What doors, windows, elevators, stairwells, or fire escapes would you use?
- Keep your purse, cell phone, and car keys in a place where you can get to them if you have to leave quickly.
- Tell your neighbors about your concerns and ask that they call the police if they hear suspicious noises coming from your house.
- Teach your children to call 911 to contact the police.
- Use a code word with your children or friends so they can call for help.

- When you expect that there is going to be an escalation in the abuse, avoid the bathroom, garage, kitchen, and other areas near weapons, or rooms without access to an outside door.
- Use your judgment and intuition. If the situation is very serious, you may decide to give your partner what he wants to calm him down. Do what you need to do to protect yourself until you are out of danger.

IF YOU ARE THINKING ABOUT LEAVING

- Consider opening up a savings account for yourself.
- Consider finding employment if you are unemployed.
- Explore employment courses through local colleges.
- Research resources in your community (e.g., the food bank).
- Speak to the staff at a women's shelter.
- Identify family and friends who will support and help you.
- Look for places to rent.
- Investigate options for social or affordable housing.
- Keep copies of important documents, keys, clothes, and money with a friend or a family member.
- Download important files from any shared computers to a portable hard drive (e.g., photos, income tax documents, contacts). Delete anything you don't want to leave on the computer.
- Keep numbers of important resources with you or memorize these numbers.

IF YOU HAVE LEFT OR YOUR PARTNER HAS LEFT

- Change the locks on doors. Install additional locks, window bars, or poles to wedge against doors.
- Consider installing a security system.

- Change passwords on important online accounts (e.g., e-mail, banking, Facebook, etc.).
- If you don't already have it, get caller ID.
- Make sure you cannot be located through your phone (turn off phone tracking).
- If you have a joint phone plan, consider getting your own phone.
- Check with your cell phone provider for other security measures.
- Teach your children how to use a phone to call you in the event your partner takes them.
- Tell the people who take care of your children that your partner is not permitted to pick them up, and provide all caregivers with a list of the individuals who can pick your children up.
- Inform neighbors and friends that your partner no longer resides with you and that they should call the police if he is seen near your home.
- Plan ahead for what you can do if you feel down and are considering going back to your partner.
- Identify friends or family members you can call for support.
- Develop a plan that best protects your safety if you have to communicate with or see your partner.

It may be overwhelming to think about all you could do to gather support or to plan for the future. Try not to get overwhelmed by taking on too much at once. Instead, ask yourself if there is one thing you could do to get more support for yourself or to plan for the future. For example, one woman realized she needed to get out of her car loan and buy a less expensive car if she was ever to be financially independent of her partner. She hadn't decided yet if she was going to separate from her partner, but she wanted to be debt-free regardless. Putting her car up for sale was an attainable step that made it more possible to leave her partner. It did not mean, however, that she had to leave him.

Women sometimes find there are things they can do that will give them more support or open up some options for them without forcing a decision about staying or leaving. Each little step you make is very significant. Some of the steps you make do not seem visible. They have to do with how you are thinking and feeling rather than what you are doing. However, women who have worked through this process tell us that some of these small steps, such as changing how they thought about themselves or their situation, made a big difference. By beginning to realize that you are in a very difficult situation and deserve some affirmation and support, you are taking a very significant step.

We have so much compassion for women living with abuse. We know it is really hard and can be very isolating. We believe you deserve as much good support as you can find for yourself. We hope this chapter has given you some helpful ideas about getting more support. Keep reaching out. You should not be alone.

In our next chapter, we will discuss the many factors you need to consider when deciding to leave, or to stay with, your abusive partner.

TEN

Should I Leave My Partner?

I thought a lot about leaving but I was torn. I still loved Michael, but his treatment of me was intolerable. I also felt I couldn't deal with the terrible embarrassment of a separation. Perhaps even more important, I was afraid to be alone. One of the impacts of Michael's abuse was that I thought poorly of myself. I thought that no other man would want to be with me. It felt like Michael was my only chance for marriage and family. I didn't want to stay in an abusive relationship, but if I left, I might be alone for the rest of my life. The whole dilemma seemed overwhelming.

—KATE

Through the process of reading this book, you have done some hard work in order to evaluate your relationship. You have explored the different ways that your partner has been abusive and the impact that his abuse has had on you and your children. A careful examination of your partner's beliefs and behaviors has perhaps made you wonder if you should leave him. This is a difficult and painful question to ask. It brings a myriad of emotional and practical concerns to the surface for you. In this chapter, we will explore this very complex question.

STAYING OR LEAVING?

We have noticed, and you probably have, too, that if you confide in anyone about your partner, their first reaction is, "Why are you still with him?" You may also have your own questions about this. If you've left the relationship, you may wonder why you stayed as long as you did.

Our society offers only two possibilities regarding relationships—staying or leaving. Either you're with your partner or you've left him. This seems to apply to all relationships, not just abusive ones. However, when women are in an abusive relationship, people seem to feel more justified in offering the simple (and naive) solution of leaving. Perhaps you yourself wonder why you remain with a partner who is not respectful.

If you are still working on a relationship with your partner—whether you are living together or separately—it might be helpful to list the reasons that you are still committed to your relationship. If you have left your partner, think back to the reasons why you stayed for the time that you did.

MY REASONS FOR STAYING

_____

_____

_____

_____

_____

_____

Women have shared with us the following reasons for staying, some of which may be on your list:

* I still love him!
* I don't want to be alone.

- I take my marriage vows very seriously.
- I want to get back what we once had.
- I still have dreams and hope for the future.
- I feel embarrassed about being abused.
- I'm worried about the effects of separation or divorce on the children.
- I share financial commitments with my partner.
- I don't know if financially and emotionally I can manage on my own.
- I'm worried that single parenting will be too hard.
- I'm feeling too exhausted or overwhelmed to make a big decision.
- I hold strong values and ideas about marriage and commitment.
- I feel strongly identified as a couple with friends, family, and my community.
- I'm afraid of disappointing my family.
- I want the children to have a father.
- I feel sorry for him.
- I don't want to lose my home.
- He's never physically abused me.
- At least he doesn't drink.
- He's threatened to kill himself.
- He's in counseling. I'm waiting to see if he changes.
- He has some redeeming qualities, which I am holding on to.
- He has threatened to hurt me if I leave with the children.
- He has threatened to get custody of the children if I leave.

Generally, women say that they want the abuse to end, not the relationship. Even if you have separated in order to gain some safety, you may be hoping that your partner will change so that you can stay together.

We recognize that living separately—whether that is establishing your own home, staying with friends or family, or going to a women's shelter or safe house for a while—doesn't necessarily mean you want to or intend to end the relationship. It means that you are attempting to establish expectations for a safe, respectful, and mutual relationship.

You are doing what you can to make sense of this relationship for yourself. When you're ready, you'll make a decision that is right for you.

WHY IS IT SO HARD EVEN TO THINK ABOUT LEAVING?

When evaluating why you stay in your relationship, it may be helpful to realize how the impact of the abuse plays a role in keeping you in the relationship. Abuse from a partner often leaves a woman feeling exhausted, overwhelmed, and confused. Deciding to leave your partner is no doubt one of the hardest decisions you will ever make. It is hard to make such a life-changing decision when you feel exhausted or paralyzed by all the abuse. Women describe a lengthy and painful process in making the decision to leave an abusive partner. They don't wake up one morning and say to themselves, "My partner is abusive and I need to leave." Women who do leave often take lots of time to think about and plan ahead for a separation.

It may also be helpful to remind yourself that any woman would find it very difficult and stressful to leave the person she thought she had committed to. Even if your partner were not abusive, it would be overwhelming to deal with all the things related to a separation (e.g., moving, effects on your children, reactions of family and friends, embarrassment, etc.). When you add to it the exhaustion, frayed nerves, and fear that come from living with an abusive man, it may seem almost impossible.

SHOULD I STAY WHILE MY PARTNER IS IN COUNSELING?

Sometimes women feel that they need to stay while their partners are in counseling. Women do this out of a sense of wanting to give their partners a "fair" chance. First of all, you probably don't need to worry about being "fair." You have likely given your partner many, many chances to change. Second, there is no reason why you can't live apart while your partner is in counseling and then, at the end of his program, assess if he has changed enough for you to want to try the relationship again. In fact, your partner may be more motivated if he realizes that the relationship is at stake if he doesn't change. In our experience, abusive men won't even attempt to change unless they believe they have something significant to lose.

Your partner may try to convince you that he's changed "enough" and that you should be grateful. We hope you'll be able to evaluate your partner's changes in terms of your own expectations (refer back to your expectation list in Chapter 7). Only you can decide whether the changes your partner has made make you feel safe and respected in your relationship. Trust yourself.

Some questions you may ask yourself to help decide whether your partner's changes are sufficient might include:

Can I make decisions about the children, money, or my own life without worrying about his reaction?

Does he demonstrate that he is concerned about my safety?

Is he still interested in being central, superior, and deserving? (For example: Does he need to be right? Make the big decisions? Act entitled?)

Does he spend quality time with the children without any conditions?

Is he still driving the Cycle of Abuse? (Do I feel safe, or am I walking on eggshells?)

For more about how to assess whether your partner is changing so that you and your children are safe, we recommend an excellent book by Lundy Bancroft, *Why Does He Do That?: Inside the Minds of Angry and Controlling Men*. Even if your partner is making lots of changes, it may not feel safe to live together. Just because he is changing, you should not feel obligated to stay.

WHY IS MY PARTNER STILL ABUSIVE EVEN THOUGH I LEFT HIM?

Unfortunately, your partner may continue the Cycle of Abuse whether you are with him or not. That is because he is still operating from a place of power and control. When a woman leaves, an abusive man can feel that he is losing his power and use the three phases of the Cycle and many tactics of abuse to try to regain his control. Let's look at one woman's story.

ELAINE

Elaine has left her partner and is hiding from him at a co-worker's house. She has wisely chosen to stay with someone her husband doesn't know. He initially tries to find her by using honeymoon behavior on her family and friends. He expresses great concern for Elaine to her parents and insists that he is willing to cooperate in whatever ways are necessary to overcome their problems. He says similar things to the rest of her family. When it becomes clear that Elaine's family is not willing to betray her, her partner moves on to tension-building behavior, pestering and harassing her family with phone calls. Finally, he explodes, smashing the windshield of her sister's car.

There seem to be numerous ways for an abusive man to continue the Cycle even if you are not with him. For example, he may use the court system, threatening to sue for custody of your children or refusing to release money or assets that he owes you. He may use visits with the children as an opportunity to abuse you, acting kind and helpful one day and exploding in front of the children the next. He may post lies about you on Facebook to humiliate you. Perhaps he harasses you at work, which threatens your employment. But as you likely realize by now, your partner used many of these tactics while you were together. They are not new; it's just that you were hopeful that once you left, the abuse would stop.

Another way that abusive men continue to be abusive after separation is through text, e-mail, or social media. Women report receiving some "honeymoon" messages—he says he regrets his actions and promises to change. Other messages reflect the tension or explosion phase—he is critical, demeaning, or threatening. This is all confusing and takes a huge emotional toll. Because most of us carry our phones with us all the time, it seems, for some women, as if their abusive ex-partner is with them all the time. For all these reasons, you may consider limiting his contact with you through text, e-mail, or social media. If it feels safe to block his number, do that. If you need to be in touch for the children, consider limiting how often you reply or respond to his messages. Maybe you can turn off your phone when you are busy with the children, at work, or going to bed. We know that sometimes it is too dangerous to ignore messages and you will need to consider whether it is safe to ignore them or delay in responding. It is good, however, to at least consider limiting his access to you in this way. Having some breaks from his abusive messages may help you to feel clearer and stronger in your own mind.

Because abusive men continue the Cycle of Abuse after separation, women have to continue to be on guard and be very thoughtful about ways to create more physical and emotional distance from their ex-partners and their abusive tactics. This can be discouraging. You would like to think that once you have left your partner, he will no longer have the ability to control or hurt you. Sadly, this is not always the case. Many women have found, however, that once they are no longer living with their partners and are no longer exposed to the constant abuse, the impact of the abuse begins to lessen. Most women feel safer and stronger when there is some distance between themselves and their partners.

WILL LEAVING AFFECT MY CHILDREN'S RELATIONSHIP WITH THEIR FATHER?

When women consider whether to stay or leave, concern about the children always plays a big role in their decision making. Women wonder how their decision may affect the children's relationship with their father. On the one hand, women who consider leaving may experience judgment from others for alienating their children from their dad. A woman may be accused of trying to damage the dad's relationship with his children, which is confusing since she is trying to protect her children. On the other hand, if a woman is currently living with her partner, she may be criticized by others for "letting" her children be exposed to abuse. We understand that you are just trying to figure out what is best for your children, but it is not always clear what is best.

We think that perhaps there is a different way to look at your situation, which we hope will bring some clarity. It may be helpful to realize that only your partner has the ability to choose whether he is a good dad or not, and his choice is not determined by whether you are living together or not. If your partner is abusing you in front of the children, you may decide to leave for the sake of your children's well-being. You are not doing this to "damage" his relationship with them; you are doing this to protect them. His behavior has made it necessary to live apart, but he can still choose to be a good dad. Whether you stay or leave, only your partner can decide what kind of father he is. The two are not tied to each other, as the story below illustrates. It is not about whether you stay or leave. It is about whether he chooses to be a good and safe dad or not.

SUSAN AND TED

Ted had been abusive to Susan for many years. Ted began attending a group for abusive men, and Susan went to a support group for women. Ted's behavior began to improve, but Susan realized that she really wanted and needed to live apart from him, at least for a while. Ted continued to attend his group and began behaving in ways that were considerate and respectful of Susan and their two children. However, over time, Susan realized that the marriage was over for her; too much damage had been done by Ted's past abusive behavior. She was not willing to live with him again. However, Susan was hopeful that Ted could be a good father to their children. Because Ted had stopped being abusive and was being respectful to Susan, the two of them worked out a reasonable custody agreement. The children now spend time with their father, who treats both them and their mother in respectful ways.

This story shows that a man can choose to be a good father whether he lives with his children or not. The choice is his. Also remember that part of being a good father is treating you well.

AM I READY TO BE A SINGLE PARENT?

You may worry about leaving your partner and trying to be a parent on your own. Being a single parent can be difficult. You may be concerned not only about the emotional pressures of single parenting but also about the financial and social pressures. There are a lot of practical matters to consider. Can you secure affordable housing? Will you have enough money to pay for groceries and meet the basic needs of the children? Will the children be able to keep their extra activities (e.g., sports and music) or will some of these extras need to go, at least for now?

Women also wonder if they can meet all the parenting needs of their children. Some women wonder if they can do it on their own. If you are living with your partner, it might be helpful to analyze how difficult your current situation is. You may already be doing most of the parenting work. Pause for a moment and think this through. Try making two lists—what you do to care for the children and what he does. Remember to record such things as housework, cooking, shopping, laundry, doctors' appointments, soccer games, trips to the library, and household scheduling.

AM I READY TO BE A SINGLE PARENT?

ME: _____   HIM: _____

_____   _____

_____   _____

_____   _____

_____   _____

In looking at your two lists, you may realize that your partner is not currently contributing very much to your children's care and well-being. If this is the case, it may be easier to think about managing on your own with your children. On the other hand, you may also realize that your partner offers some important and valuable things to your children. If this is the case, remember Ted and Susan's story: Living apart from your partner does not negate his ability to be a good parent.

It is also helpful to remember that dealing with an abusive partner is exhausting. You may feel at the end of your rope and decide you couldn't possibly survive as a single parent. But your exhaustion is due largely to your partner's abuse. If you weren't so tired and stressed out from the abuse, the responsibilities of parenting would not seem so overwhelming. This can be difficult to see when you are living with the abuse or dealing with it on an ongoing basis.

WHAT IF I DON'T WANT MY CHILDREN TO SEE THEIR FATHER?

Common belief says that children should maintain contact with their father, but this is not always the case. Rather than holding on to this generalization, think about your particular situation. If your partner abuses your children or his abuse of you affects them negatively, then you have good reason to want to limit his contact. You are being a good mother and are attempting to protect your children from abuse.

You may not have the final say on whether your partner will have access to your children. Courts are hesitant to limit a father's access to his children. You may find yourself fighting for limited or no access and having few allies. You may be made to feel selfish or vindictive. Sometimes women get accused by the courts of being "uncooperative" or "alienating the father" when they are really just trying to protect their children. If you have been accused of such things, consider again your motives. If your concern is for the welfare of your children, do not feel bad. Remember, you know your children and your family situation better than anyone else; you are the expert on the welfare of your children.

If you share children with your abusive partner, you are facing a very difficult and painful reality. Like it or not, you have a link with your partner that will last at least until your children are grown. Your partner may try to maintain control over you through your children. Fighting for custody or failing to provide support payments is a powerful way to hurt you and maintain power over you.

Perhaps the biggest fear for most women is the fear of losing their children. They are afraid that they will either lose custody of their children or lose their children's respect and love. In working with women, we have witnessed that, when it comes to parenting, the long-term matters. Your partner may try to win your children's favor by buying expensive gifts. He may tell lies about you that your children believe for a while. These are painful experiences. But your partner will not be a consistently "good" parent. You can be a source of stability for your children. You can be dependable, predictable, loving, honest, and respectful. For most children, this is what matters in the long run.

We hope this chapter has addressed some of the questions you have as you consider whether or not to leave your partner. We also hope we have honored how truly painful the question is. We know that it is never an easy decision. It is not our intention to convince you to leave. We believe that you are in the best position to make that decision for yourself. None of us can make that judgment for each other. You will make the decision at your own pace and in your own way. You know what is best for you—and what is safest.

ELEVEN

How Do I Heal from the Abuse?

For several days I had been feeling really strong and happy. I had thought very little about my ex-partner. But then I took our daughter to the pool for a swim. I saw all those moms and dads together with their kids, and sadness flooded over me. I saw in those families what I had always wanted for my daughter and me. It feels discouraging. How much longer am I going to feel all this pain? When am I going to feel like I'm really getting on with my life?

—JESSICA

WHY DOES THIS HURT SO MUCH?

While each woman's journey to wholeness after the devastating experience of abuse is unique, there are some important similarities. The healing process tends to involve periods of intense grief and sadness as well as periods of rebuilding and hope. These two experiences may feel unrelated, but for us, they are two sides of a coin; they go together. This will become clearer as you read this chapter. Let's begin by talking about the grieving part of the healing process.

IS GRIEVING PART OF THE HEALING PROCESS?

A woman leaving, or considering leaving, an abusive partner moves through a process of grief that can be complex and challenging. You may find yourself overwhelmed with painful feelings of sadness and loss. This is grief. Your life is not the way you imagined it would be, and if you have children, many of your hopes and dreams for them may not have come true either. Added to the many and complex emotions you are experiencing is the reality that you feel alone in your pain. You may have kept many of your feelings to yourself because your friends and family do not understand what you are going through, and are unable to offer the support you need and deserve.

In our society, we are given permission to grieve the death of a parent, a child, or a spouse. People will offer emotional and practical support to allow loved ones to grieve and heal. Other losses such as divorce, however, go unrecognized, especially if a woman is leaving an abusive partner. For the most part, people do not recognize the grieving process that people experience when they separate or divorce. They may think that when a marriage "doesn't work," both parties choose to separate. Even if it is recognized as a significant loss, society does not create much opportunity for grieving. Yet from our perspective, separation and divorce can be painful and grief is normal.

Janette's story illustrates some of these additional complexities, and it highlights similarities and differences between different endings to two different relationships.

JANETTE

I lost my first husband to kidney failure. It was horrible. He was sick for a long time before he died, and when he was finally gone, I was devastated. My family and church community were wonderful, however. I was allowed to be an emotional wreck. I cried a lot. People took my kids so I could have time to myself. Friends were always bringing over food—our fridge was full of home-cooked meals, cookies, and cakes. Losing my husband this way was really awful, but my community saw me through it, and after many months, the pain and loss I felt began to lift.

My second marriage, in contrast, ended because my husband was abusive. Compared to the death of my first husband, the grief was just as bad, but it was much more complicated. I was very confused for a long time, and it was all very messy. Before I left for good, I went back to my husband many times, so there was no clear break. My children (now grown) became very judgmental of me. They wanted me out of the relationship and could not understand why I kept going back. I loved my husband. I wanted the relationship to work out. I wanted the abuse to end, not the relationship.

When I finally decided the relationship was over, I was devastated, but no one, except the women in my support group, could understand my grief. Some people thought I should have left my husband long ago and thought I should "just be happy to be out." Others judged me for ending my marriage and had no sympathy for my painfully difficult decision.

My two experiences of grief were so entirely different. With the death of my second marriage, I was expected to swallow my pain. There was no formal recognition of my loss (something that a funeral provides), and no one brought casseroles or homemade cookies.

As Janette's story illustrates, sometimes a woman's grief is minimized, and her loss is not recognized.

People say things like "she chose to leave," or "he was so terrible, she should be glad to be out." Other times, women are judged for choosing to end a relationship and consequently do not get the support that they need. Judgments may include "he never hit her," "he seemed like such a good guy," "he didn't cheat on her," "he was so involved with his children," or "it didn't seem that bad." Your losses, and the grieving process that goes with them, tend not to be socially recognized. This can be very painful for women, particularly during a time when they need the care and support of friends, family, and helping professionals.

On top of this, because your partner is abusive, there may be added dimensions to your loss. For example, women usually lose contact with their in-laws (who are sometimes as dear to them as their own relatives). They are also likely to lose former friends who believe their ex-partner's lies. Furthermore, because financial abuse is often present, there can be tremendous financial impacts such as losing a home or falling into debt.

It may be sad for you to realize that women in your situation have many things to grieve. Here is a list of some things that women say about their grief:

- I grieve the loss of who I thought my husband was.
- I no longer trust the person I thought I could trust the most.
- I grieve the death of my hopes and dreams.
- My life is not at all how I wanted it to be.
- My family, as I knew it, is gone.
- I have my children only 50 percent of the time.
- I lost the opportunity to be a "stay-at-home mom." I have to work.
- My children turned against me.
- I lost my home and my garden.
- I lost most of my friends and my faith community.
- I've lost social status.
- I feel labeled: "divorced," "single mom," "broken home."
- I lost all sense of financial security.
- I feel like I've lost the best years of my life.

- I'm feeling the loss of opportunities (education, career, etc.).
- I've lost everything!

If your relationship has ended or is ending, your losses are enormous. The grief and pain you feel may seem too much to bear at times, and if you are like most women in your situation, your community may not understand or offer support to you while you grieve. You may also not understand or recognize all your own losses. Remember that if you are contemplating leaving your partner, or have already done so, you are probably going through one of the most painful periods of your life. We hope that you are receiving the support and understanding that you need, considering all your losses.

WHY IS IT HARD TO GRIEVE?

We know that grief can be a lengthy and painful process that follows any significant loss. It is normal for us to grieve all sorts of things, such as the loss of an enjoyable job or a loss of health. Likewise, the end of any significant relationship requires time to grieve. However, there are many reasons why women leaving abusive relationships may be prevented from expressing their grief.

Sometimes women feel "frozen" in their grief for a time. That is, they have to postpone their grieving for one or several reasons. We know that just because a woman leaves, it does not mean that the abuse ends. So you may have to put off grieving in order to stay emotionally tough and fight to protect yourself, your children, or your financial security. In this case, the person whose loss you are grieving continues to hurt you; you may find yourself swinging from extreme sadness at your losses to extreme anger with each new assault from your ex-partner.

In the following example, Frances describes how she feels. "I'm just trying to survive . . . I can't tend to my wounds because I am still in the battle."

When I left my relationship, my partner immediately began legal action against me. He tried to prove in court that I was an unfit parent. I had to fight with everything that I had to protect my infant son. In the midst of such a momentous battle, there was no time to grieve that my marriage was over. I was angry, and I was scared, but it wasn't until the court process was over that I could feel sad for all my losses. (Happily, I was successful in court and my ex-partner's claims were exposed as lies.)

—FRANCES

You may also be unable to grieve because you are overwhelmed with practical concerns. You may have to find a new home, get a job, or find child care. These things would be challenging under any circumstances, but after an abusive relationship, they are even more difficult. Fear, fatigue, lack of support, financial stress, and poor health are just some of the things that may be contributing to your sense of being overwhelmed.

Our society's expectations in such a situation are quite unrealistic. Would we expect a hostage victim, after years of captivity, to immediately go and find a job, rent a new home, buy a car, and fill the cupboards with groceries? Probably not. We would provide such a person with support and time to heal; we would recognize the terrible emotional cost of the experience and allow for recovery. Similarly, what a woman leaving abuse really needs is time to heal, grieve, and gather her strength, but that is not usually what she gets. Most women feel like all they are doing is "surviving" for the first year or so after separation. They don't have the time or emotional energy to tally all their losses. The daily demands of life leave little space for personal reflection and healing. And if they have children, they may find themselves prioritizing their children's emotional needs over their own.

Sometimes, a long time after the separation, unexpected feelings of sadness sweep over women. Suddenly they can feel quite overwhelmed by their losses. Unfortunately, by this time some family and friends think that they should be "over it" and women do not receive the care and support they need.

I HAVEN'T LEFT MY PARTNER, SO WHY DO I FEEL LIKE I'M GRIEVING?

Some women tell us that they experienced grief while they were still with their partner. You may have never thought about some of your feelings of sadness and anger as grief. You have experienced a lot of losses. Your relationship is not the way you want it to be. If you have children, they do not have the kind of father you would want for them. It is natural and normal for you to feel sad for all the things that are not going as you had planned. It makes for a complicated sort of grief if the losses come over years, while you are still in the relationship.

The death of my marriage was gradual, over many years. Mark's hateful behavior was like a cancer that gradually killed my love for him. Mark didn't die, but my love for him sure did. It was a slow and painful process, and I was aware of grieving a lot while I was still with him. I would think things like, "Well, I guess this is all that I can expect," and feel very sad that my marriage was not what I wanted it to be.

—JODY

In some ways, Jody's description of her grief is like that of a person who loses a loved one to a disease like Alzheimer's. It is gradual, slow, and very painful. The losses come over time and a lot of the grieving happens while the person is still alive. In a similar way, women gradually lose their hopes and dreams for their relationship. Maybe you can relate to some of Jody's experience? The losses accumulate while you are still together; remember, women do a lot of grieving while still in the relationship. Grief is not tied to leaving. If you have been confused about why you have been feeling so sad, maybe it's that you are grieving your losses. So much of your life and the life you imagined for your children is not what you hoped it would be.

WHY DO I HAVE SUCH MIXED EMOTIONS ABOUT THE END OF MY RELATIONSHIP?

As we have seen in this chapter, although grief can be very powerful and consuming, you may also be experiencing periods of hope and excitement about a future that is free from abuse. We want you to feel hopeful that by experiencing both the painful emotions of grief and the positive feelings of rebuilding, you can heal from the abuse.

In our experience, most women find the first few years after separation to be a roller coaster of confusing emotions. Sometimes they feel all the losses of the relationship while other times they are relieved and happy to have left. It is normal to experience a diverse range of emotions. In fact, moving through various thoughts and feelings is a key component to healing from the abuse you have experienced.

For many women, the healing process includes both grieving and moving forward: sometimes feeling and naming all the losses they have experienced, and at other times rebuilding their lives. We would like to share a diagram that illustrates and describes what the healing process might look like for you. As with most things that have to do with our emotions, real life is not as neat and tidy as the diagram. You may spend hours and even days in the rebuilding part of the process and then, suddenly, find yourself swept back into grief. Similarly, you may be spending a great deal of time in grief, feeling many powerful and uncomfortable emotions, and then, without warning, feel great joy or hope at the smallest of things. As life evolves, many women begin to feel more positive and even joyful in their newfound freedom and independence. We think that the examples we provide in the "Rebuilding" and "Grieving" sections will help you to make sense of all the mixed emotions you have been experiencing in your healing journey and offer you hope for your future.

DIAGRAM 11.1: THE HEALING PROCESS

The top part of the figure, titled "Rebuilding," is the part of the healing process when you are moving forward and feeling more hopeful about your future. The abuse has taken so much away from you, and here you are rebuilding that which your partner tore down.

Here are some things that women tell us they experience during these times. Check off the emotions that fit for you.

Rebuilding Emotions

○ I feel hopeful.

○ I feel strong.

○ I feel at peace.

○ I feel safe (or safer).

○ I feel "normal."

○ I feel relief.

○ I feel energized.

○ I feel euphoric at times.

○ I experience joy.

○ I feel cheerful.

○ I feel affirmed.

○ I feel good about myself.

○ I feel rejuvenated.

○ I feel positive.

○ I think more clearly.

○ I am excited about my future.

○ I feel beautiful.

○ I am able to make decisions.

○ I am optimistic.

○ I have more clarity.

○ I see possibilities.

○ I feel more in control.

○ I feel more confident.

○ I trust myself.

○ I trust my instincts.

○ I like myself.

○ I am finding out who I am.

○ I am rediscovering myself.

○ I am angry.

○ _____

○ _____

○ _____

We hope that you are experiencing some of these life-affirming emotions, even if they come only in short bursts. Many women, in the time immediately following a separation, experience these more positive emotions only in small amounts, as there are many things that may push you back into the grieving part of the healing process. Getting relief from your sadness for short periods of time may give you hope that you will find joy and happiness again and you can start to believe that you will be okay. It will not always be this hard.

If you look back at the diagram, you will notice that the bottom part of the loop is labeled "Grieving." Women report to us that, as they move through this part of the process, they experience some of the emotions listed below. Check off those that fit for you.

Grieving Emotions

○ I feel that things are hopeless.

○ I feel helpless.

○ I am afraid for myself.

○ I am afraid for my children.

○ I worry about the long-term impact on my children.

○ I regret my children are not having the life I want for them.

○ I have no appetite.

○ I feel nauseous.

○ I grieve for the friends I have lost.

○ I worry about losing more friends.

○ I can't get off the couch or out of bed.

○ I have trouble making decisions.

○ I feel hurt.

○ I am sad.

○ I feel my heart is breaking.

○ I grieve for the loss of what I thought my future was going to look like.

○ I am lonely.

○ I feel like a failure.

○ I am frustrated.

○ I experience regret.

○ I feel responsible.

○ I have intrusive thoughts.

○ I can't stop wondering how it could have been different.

○ I feel guilty.

○ I feel shame.

○ I am afraid to trust people.

○ I feel betrayed by family and friends.

○ I feel unsettled and in a constant state of transition.

○ I feel confused.

○ I feel like I am only enduring life.

○ I see no possibilities.

○ I am depressed.

○ I feel like I am suffocating.

○ I grieve for the family I have lost (his family, too).

○ I worry about money.

○ I fear that I will never have a good relationship with a man.

○ I feel anxious.   ○ I am angry.
○ I am exhausted.   ○ _____
○ I feel overwhelmed.   ○ _____
○ I have poor health.   ○ _____

We have put an opening at the top and the bottom of the figure eight, a reminder that someday you will move out of this intense emotional process.

You may also have times when you are in neither part of this figure eight. We spoke earlier about frozen grief, and this may be what is happening for you. Sometimes you may feel so overwhelmed by your situation that you "numb out" from many of your emotions both positive and painful. In the days immediately after leaving her partner, Cate wrote in her journal, "There are so many thoughts in my head. I can't process them all, so I won't process any of them. I am shutting down."

There are all kinds of things that may cause you to "shut down." If you are fearful for your life, fighting in court for your children, or living with a high level of stress, you may feel that all you can do is survive.

Once again, be kind to yourself. We believe that there are times when "surviving the day" shows immense courage and determination. Also, it is our experience that once you are out of this intense period of crisis, you will have emotional energy for your healing process.

WHY AM I SO ANGRY?

You will notice that anger appears in both of the preceding lists. How is it that you may be feeling anger in both the rebuilding and the grieving phases of the healing process? We believe that anger plays an important role in healing and that there is more than one type of anger. Some anger may feel energizing. It may help you to "stay strong" and "fight" for what is right. It is an anger that propels you forward to build a better life. Many women find that, if they can harness this anger, it can be a powerful fuel for accomplishing the difficult tasks ahead of them.

There is also anger that is more associated with grief. As women add up all the losses in their lives, they feel angry. They feel they have been robbed. It is very difficult to know what to do with this anger. You are, in fact, angry at your partner and all the damage he has caused you, but it is not safe to express your anger toward him. You may also feel angry with people or institutions that have let you down, but there is usually little you can do to right these wrongs. Consequently, some women describe the anger as "simmering" inside them. This type of anger tends to be more immobilizing and oppressive, and sometimes women feel paralyzed by it. Other times, women are afraid of the rage they feel building up inside them and worry about what they might be capable of doing. It is important to let yourself experience this very justified anger and find safe places to talk about it. Try writing in a journal or joining a women's support group. These are all important parts of the healing process.

You may also find it hard to feel angry. You may be feeling a new level of anger, some of your feelings and thoughts may be frightening, and many of us have been raised with the message that women should not be angry. Furthermore, your abusive partner demonstrated how harmful anger can be. Remember that anger is not the problem. It is a normal, healthy human emotion. Given all the ways you have been hurt, it is appropriate to feel angry. The challenge becomes what to do with that anger. As we said before, whenever possible, try to use your anger to empower you to take steps toward a better life.

When your anger is more disempowering, acknowledge it as part of the healing process, and try to find a helpful way to express it. Anger is not generally pleasant, but you will be glad to know that it doesn't last forever. In our experience, the intense and sometimes frightening level of anger you may be feeling now will subside over time.

IS THERE SOMETHING WRONG WITH ME?

Healing from the kinds of losses you have experienced is messy. Many women fear that they might be "going crazy." We don't think you are going crazy; in fact, we think you are doing important emotional work no matter what part of the figure eight you are spending most of your time in.

The intense grief you are experiencing may lead you to see a counselor. Hopefully, that counselor understands your experience and is supportive. However, you may be seeing someone who hasn't made the connection between your complicated grief, all the impacts of abuse, and your feelings of depression, fear, and fatigue. Some counselors or support people might label you with a mental health problem such as depression or anxiety. What is really being named are some of the impacts of abuse. Sometimes a woman does find it helpful to take medication for a while, but it is important to remember you are having a normal human reaction to external circumstances.

Similarly, your physical health may be affected as you work through this intense healing process. Chest pains, stomach problems, headaches, insomnia, and chronic fatigue are all examples of physical ailments that women sometimes experience as they process what has happened to them. While you don't want to ignore these physical symptoms and should have them checked by your doctor, most women find that they subside over time.

Unfortunately, you may find that many people in your life, while able to support you in the rebuilding part of the process, will criticize you for grieving. Many women are accused of not "moving on," and they may even be told that there is something wrong with them. On any given day, at any given moment, whether you are grieving or rebuilding, you are on the journey of healing. Take time to recognize your strength and honor yourself for the hard emotional work that you are doing.

WHY DOES THE END OF A "BAD" RELATIONSHIP STILL HURT SO MUCH?

As we have said, sometimes friends, family, neighbors, employers, and others do not understand the pain you may be going through. They think you should just be happy to be out of a "bad" relationship. Remember that what you are in the middle of is an immensely complex healing process.

While you are grieving, you may begin to recognize impacts and wounds from your ex-partner's abuse. Meanwhile, the abuse may be ongoing, and there may be new impacts.

It is helpful to remind yourself that in most other situations, when we grieve, it is because of the end of something. Someone has died or we have lost our home or our job. In this case, there is no clear-cut termination. Your partner hasn't died; rather, he very likely continues to hurt you on an almost daily basis. (This is particularly true if you have children.) There is no closure but rather a continual rewounding. It is also very likely that you will remember your partner's "good qualities" after leaving the relationship. After reading this book, you may realize that his apparent kindness and goodness were often a means of manipulating you; it was part of the honeymoon.

Still, that goodness felt authentic to you at the time, and of course, most men who are abusive do have positive qualities. You would never have stayed with him if this were not the case. And so, perhaps you remember the "good times" you had together and feel a longing for what you have lost.

Because the healing process you are moving through is so complex and intense, you are at a particularly vulnerable time in your life. Many women feel like their emotions are scattered all over the place. Both grieving and rebuilding take an enormous amount of emotional energy. We think it is important to be aware of your potential vulnerability. For this reason, we usually caution women against beginning a new relationship while they are still healing. Friends and family may encourage you to "get back out there and date," but trust your instincts and give yourself the time you need to heal from all that you have suffered.

IS IT ALWAYS GOING TO BE THIS PAINFUL?

Healing from your relationship is a long process. We don't say this to discourage you but hopefully to reassure that what you are experiencing is normal. Despite your fears, you are not crazy for feeling intense and divergent emotions. Many women despair at how long the grieving process takes. You want it to be over so you can get on with your life. You want it to "be done." We hope it is helpful to know that this process of rebuilding and grieving does take a long time, but it won't always be this painful. You are doing crucial emotional healing work.

Women tell us over and over again that it does get better. In time you will find your emotions less intense and your mind less consumed by this process. Women who have been free of abuse for some time report having days when they "feel normal" again.

Also, the healing process itself will alter over time. Early on, many women spend the majority of their time in grief. This is natural for anyone experiencing a significant loss. Eventually, however, most women tell us that they spend more time rebuilding. After years of being "shut down" by their partner's controlling behavior, women find great joy in exploring new relationships and experiences. Sometimes women learn new things about themselves. Some women discover gifts and abilities they never knew they had.

If you have been separated for quite a while, you may be spending much of your time in the rebuilding part of the figure eight. However, you will likely find that there are a number of "triggering events" that will pull you back into the grief. Women report to us that sights, smells, and memories will trigger grief for them. Major events such as birthdays and anniversaries can be very painful. Holidays such as Thanksgiving and Christmas, that emphasize the importance of family, can bring great waves of sadness because your family is not the way you hoped it would be. Events within your extended family may also do this. For example, a wedding or a funeral that puts you in the same room as your ex-partner can be difficult.

There is no right or wrong way to heal from all that you have experienced. Some days you will feel overjoyed to be "free" of the relationship. Other days you will feel very sad as you identify yet another thing that you have lost. Be patient with yourself and try to surround yourself with people who understand what a long and complex journey you are on. Finally, be assured that you will get through this. We have had the pleasure of working with hundreds of women over many years. We have been privileged to watch these women grow in new and exciting ways, creating rich and meaning-ful lives for themselves. You will, too!

CAN I LOOK FORWARD WITH HOPE?

We conclude our book with five stories from women who have found reasons to be hopeful. Their stories help us to see that hope takes different forms in different situations. If not today, then someday soon you, too, will be able to share a story of hope.

I only left my partner a few months ago, but I already feel much clearer and stronger. I really couldn't see just how bad things were until I got out and had a taste of what it means not to live on edge all the time.

—GILLIAN

Living with Brian for twenty-two years left me a shell of a person. He destroyed my sense of self. I felt unlovable and unacceptable. I doubted everything about myself. Separation and divorce has been hard and is still hard. I've spent a lot of money on lawyers, and I've struggled to help my family and friends understand. But as hard as it's been, I am so glad that I left when I did. I have slowly come alive as a person. I make my own decisions and have control over my life. One thing I would want to tell other women is, "It gets better!" As challenging as my life is, it is so much better than it was before.

—MARCIA

I am very thankful that my husband is changing. I know that doesn't happen often. It has taken years for him to rebuild my trust, but now I experience a lot of comfort and security. At the same time, I have worked all along to strengthen myself. Reading this book, finding a great support group, and putting safeguards in place allowed me to stay while he did the work he needed to do. I feel hopeful about our future together, but I am also certain beyond a doubt that I will never go back to the way we once were. I hope our marriage will survive and grow stronger and stronger, but at the same time I know now that I will be okay whatever happens.

—SYLVIA

I left Sean three years ago, and I am now in a loving and respectful relationship with a new person. He is so completely different from my first partner. I never really realized what I was missing out on until I got it. Glen always keeps my best interests in mind. He accepts me and appreciates me for who I am. We are best friends. We can talk about anything. He is real, faithful, and honest, and he treats me like an equal. My spirit feels at peace when I am with him.

—JULIE

I regret ever meeting Ryan, but I sure don't regret leaving him. As painful and hard as all this has been, I am glad I am finally "out." I feel like I have myself back. Once again, I know who I am. I feel strong. I can dream my own dreams and think my own thoughts. I feel like I have a future with hope.

—CAROL

AFTERWORD

For many years, women have shared their stories with us. In turn, in the pages of this book, we have shared their stories with you. We truly appreciate the gift they have given us. Each woman's story is a treasure—a witness to her strength, courage, and wisdom. We have used parts of their stories throughout our book because the truth about violence against women lies in the stories of the women themselves. For us, abuse against women is not a theory or a social phenomenon; it is what happens to real women. Although each woman's story is unique, there are remarkable similarities in the experiences, thoughts, and feelings of women when the person they love abuses them. They wrestle with the same dilemmas and confusions.

We hope that what you have read in this book has reassured you that you are truly not alone. There are others who can understand and appreciate the overwhelming situation in which you find yourself.

We also hope that this book has helped you to begin to trust your own story and to honor your own strength, courage, and wisdom.

THE AUTHORS

Karen McAndless-Davis (on the left) and Jill Cory (on the right)

Find more information and resources
at whenlovehurts.ca.